Nonprofit Compensation and Benefits Practices

Nonprofit Law, Finance, and Management Series

The Art of Planned Giving: Understanding Donors and the Culture of Giving by Douglas E. White

Beyond Fund Raising: New Strategies for Nonprofit Investment and Innovation by Kay Grace

Charity, Advocacy, and the Law by Bruce R. Hopkins

The Complete Guide to Nonprofit Management by Smith, Bucklin & Associates

Critical Issues in Fund Raising edited by Dwight Burlingame

Developing Affordable Housing: A Practical Guide for Nonprofit Organizations by Bennett L. Hecht

Financial and Accounting Guide for Not-for-Profit Organizations, Fifth Edition by Malvern J. Gross, Jr., Richard F. Larkin, Roger S. Bruttomesso, John J. McNally, Price Waterhouse LLP

Financial Planning for Nonprofit Organizations by Jody Blazek

Financial Management for Nonprofit Organizations by Jo Ann Hankin, Alan Seidner, and John Zeitlow

Fund-Raising: Evaluating and Managing the Fund Development Process by James M. Greenfield

Fund-Raising Fundamentals: A Guide to Annual Giving for Professionals and Volunteers by James M. Greenfield

Fund-Raising Regulation: A State-by-State Handbook of Registration Forms, Requirements, and Procedures by Seth Perlman and Betsy Hills Bush

Intermediate Sanctions: Curbing Nonprofit Abuse by Bruce R. Hopkins and D. Benson Tesdahl

International Guide to Nonprofit Law by Lester A. Salamon and Stefan Toepler & Associates

The Law of Fund-Raising, Second Edition by Bruce R. Hopkins

The Law of Tax-Exempt Healthcare Organizations by Thomas K. Hyatt and Bruce R. Hopkins

The Law of Tax-Exempt Organizations, Sixth Edition by Bruce R. Hopkins

The Legal Answer Book for Nonprofit Organizations by Bruce R. Hopkins

A Legal Guide to Starting and Managing a Nonprofit Organization, Second Edition by Bruce R. Hopkins

Managing Affordable Housing: A Practical Guide to Creating Stable Communities by Bennett L. Hecht, Local Initiatives Support Corporation, and James Stockard

Nonprofit Boards: Roles, Responsibilities, and Performance by Diane J. Duca

Nonprofit Compensation and Benefits Practices by Applied Research and Development Institute International, Inc.

The Nonprofit Counsel by Bruce R. Hopkins

The Nonprofit Guide to the Internet by Robbin Zeff

The Nonprofit Law Dictionary by Bruce R. Hopkins

Nonprofit Litigation: A Practical Guide with Forms and Checklists by Steve Bachmann

The Nonprofit Handbook, Second Edition: Volume I—Management by Tracy Daniel Connors

The Nonprofit Handbook, Second Edition: Volume II—Fund Raising by Jim Greenfield

The Nonprofit Manager's Resource Dictionary by Ronald A. Landskroner

Nonprofit Organizations' Business Forms: Disk Edition by John Wiley & Sons, Inc.

Partnerships and Joint Ventures Involving Tax-Exempt Organizations by Michael I. Sanders

Planned Giving: Management, Marketing, and Law by Ronald R. Jordan and Katelyn L. Quynn

Private Foundations: Tax Law and Compliance by Bruce R. Hopkins and Jody Blazek

Program Related Investments: A Technical Manual for Foundations by Christie I. Baxter

Reengineering Your Nonprofit Organization: A Guide to Strategic Transformation by Alceste T. Pappas

Reinventing the University: Managing and Financing Institutions of Higher Education by Sandra L. Johnson and Sean C. Rush, Coopers & Lybrand, L.L.P.

Strategic Planning for Nonprofit Organizations: A Practical Guide and Workbook by Michael Allison and Jude Kaye, Support Center for Nonprofit Management

Streetsmart Financial Basics for Nonprofit Managers by Thomas A. McLaughlin

A Streetsmart Guide to Nonprofit Mergers and Networks by Thomas A. McLaughlin

Successful Marketing Strategies for Nonprofit Organizations by Barry J. McLeish

The Tax Law of Charitable Giving by Bruce R. Hopkins

The Tax Law of Colleges and Universities by Bertrand M. Harding

Tax Planning and Compliance for Tax-Exempt Organizations: Forms, Checklists, Procedures, Second Edition by Jody Blazek

The Universal Benefits of Volunteering: A Practical Workbook for Nonprofit Organizations, Volunteers, and Corporations by Walter P. Pidgeon, Jr.

The Volunteer Management Handbook by Tracy Daniel Connors

Nonprofit Compensation and Benefits Practices

Carol L. Barbeito and Jack P. Bowman

Applied Research and Development
Institute International, Inc.

John Wiley & Sons, Inc.

New York • Chichester • Weinheim • Brisbane • Singapore • Toronto

This publication is designed to provide accurate and authoritative information in regard to the subject matter covered. It is sold with the understanding that the publisher is not engaged in rendering professional services. If professional advice or other expert assistance is required, the services of a competent professional person should be sought.

Library of Congress Cataloging in Publication Data:
Applied Research and Development Institute International, Inc.
    Nonprofit compensation and benefits practices / Applied Research and Development Institute International, Inc.
        p.   cm. — (Nonprofit law, finance, and management series)
    Includes bibliographical references and index.
    ISBN 0-471-18089-0 (cloth: alk. paper)
    1. Chief executive officers—Salaries, etc.—United States.
2. Executives—Salaries, etc.—United States. 3. Nonprofit organizations—Employees—Salaries, etc.—United States.
    4. Employee fringe benefits—United States.   I. Title.   II. Series.
HD4965.3.N652U63 1998
331.2'81658048—dc21   97-35611

Printed in the United States of America

10 9 8 7 6 5 4 3 2 1

Contents

Foreword   xi
Acknowledgments   xv

Chapter One   Introduction   **1**
Background   1
Understanding the Context for Compensation Programs   4
References   5

**Chapter Two: Workforce, Employment, and
Nonprofit Sector Trends**   **7**
Workforce Trends and Demographics   8
Employment Trends   8
Nonprofit Sector Trends and Demographics   10
References   12

Chapter Three: Compensation Trends   **13**
Trends in Cross-Sector Compensation Practices   14
   Compensation Strategies   14
   Benefits   17
Motivating Employees   22
How Cross-Sector Compensation Practices Are
     Affecting the Nonprofit Sector   22
References   27

**Chapter Four: Cross-Sector Study of Wages
and Benefits**   **31**
Methodology of Cross-Sector Wage-and-Benefit Study   31
   Common Benchmark Positions   32
   Other Comparison Factors   33
   Survey Data Used in This Study   34
   How the Data Was Analyzed   36

Results—Cross-Sector Salary Analysis and Comparisons   37
  Cross-Sector Comparison Summary   37
  Individual Position Comparisons   41
Results—Cross-Sector Benefits Analysis and Comparison   62
  Health Benefits   64
  Life and Disability Benefits   66
  Leave Benefits   68
  Retirement Benefits   71
  Other Benefits   73
Summary   75
References   76

**Chapter Five: Innovative Compensation
Practices in the Nonprofit Sector   79**
The Need for Information on Innovative
    Compensation Practices   79
Methodology of Study on Innovative
    Compensation Practices   80
Definitions   81
  Cash-Compensation or Recognition Plans   82
  Benefit Plans   84
Analysis and Findings   84
  Participant Profile   85
  General Plan Information   87
  Innovative Cash Compensation or Recognition Plans   89
  Positive Results of Implementing Innovative Cash
    Compensation or Recognition Plans   97
  Issues as a Result of Implementing Innovative Cash
    Compensation and Recognition Plans   99
  Innovative Benefit Plans   101
  Positive Results of Implementing Innovative Benefit Plan(s) 105
Case Studies   108
  Case Study 1: Management Incentive Plan   108
  Case Study 2: Discretionary Bonus Plan   112
  Case Study 3: Spot Award Plan   114
  Case Study 4: Noncash Recognition Plan   117
References   119

Chapter Six: Moving to Implementation   121
Roles and Relationships   125
Steps in Establishing a Compensation Policy   126
Special Considerations   136

Formulating the Compensation Plan   141
References   144

Chapter Seven: Where to Go for Further Help   147
Resources That Include Guidelines and Sample
      Compensation Policies   148
Wage-and-Benefit Surveys   149
Resources That Provide Information on Related
      Personnel Issues   153
Training and Consultation Sources   155

Appendix A
Nonprofit Management and Leadership Taxonomy   157
      Advocacy   157
      Ethics   157
      Evaluation   158
      Financial Management   158
      General Leadership   159
      General Management   159
      Governance   159
      Human Resource Management   159
      Information Systems   160
      Legal   160
      Marketing   161
      Operations Management   161
      Organization, Design, and Structure   162
      Planning   162
      Resource Development   163

Appendix B   **165**
New Legislation   165
      What You Need to Know for Your Organization   165
      401(k) Plans   165
      SIMPLE Plans   166
      Other Provisions Affecting Nonprofits   167
      How Will These Changes Affect You?   168

Appendix C   **169**
Executive Compensation by Charitable Organizations:
      A Legal Perspective   169
      Public Concern   170

    Statutory Framework   171
    Intermediate Sanctions   173
    Conclusion   176
References   177

Appendix D   **179**

Glossary   **182**

Bibliography   **188**

Index   **199**

Foreword

This very timely volume addresses the vital topic of nonprofit compensation management—the subject of immense popular distortion and of great confusion for nonprofit boards and staff members. We lack good information about current compensation policies and practices, and we also lack useful tools and management resources to help achieve more effective practice. This handy reference provides both. It offers a clear, comprehensive picture of current reality and also a practical set of tools.

Two kinds of recent events underscore the need for this book. First, the well-publicized scandals about nonprofit management focus in part on the inappropriately high salaries paid to some top executives—of United Way of America, Adelphi University, and other organizations. A national survey by Independent Sector in 1997 reports widespread public concern that some nonprofit executives are paid too much. At the same time the mass media pay scant attention to the much more pervasive reality that nonprofit executive and staff salaries are comparatively low. This sorry truth simply is not a story, although to the million nonprofits in the United States it is an extraordinarily important fact of life. Second, each year tens of thousands of nonprofits wrestle with hard choices about compensation and feel particular uncertainty about how to proceed. For example: What should we pay our executive director or a program head? What benefits packages do we need to offer in order to recruit and retain staff and in order to treat them fairly?

This study by the Applied Research and Development Institute (ARDI) documents the lower salary levels provided by the nonprofit sector, as compared to those of government agencies and for-profit organizations. Specifically, the nonprofit sector pays lower salaries in five of eight basic job categories—executive director, deputy director, department director, office manager, and secretary. This study also reports on continuing gender disparities in nonprofit compensation and on variations among regions and among different sizes of nonprofit organizations.

ARDI's examination of benefits packages presents an improving but decidedly mixed picture: nonprofits' health benefits compare favorably with those provided by other sectors, but nonprofits offer less generous medical coverage for retirees. Nonprofits' life insurance benefits compare unfavorably, yet their accidental death and long-term disability benefits are on a par with those of government and for-profit firms. Nonprofit leave policies are better than those of for-profit organizations and similar to those of government agencies.

The chapters that follow also describe the innovative compensation practices that are being used by an increasing number of nonprofits—a variety of individual and group incentive plans, bonuses, gain sharing and spot-award approaches, special cash and noncash recognition strategies, lump-sum increases, and skill-based pay. In addition, the authors present current experience with benefits, including day care, dependent care, flexible spending accounts, flextime, job-sharing, and premium conversion plans.

In its organization, content, level of detail, and practical orientation, this report should be useful to staff and board members of the broad and varied nonprofit sector and to management support organizations and consultants who advise nonprofits. It will be helpful also to others who observe and influence nonprofits—including government regulators and journalists.

This volume promises to benefit individual organizations and also the nonprofit sector as a whole. It will help nonprofits to enhance their staff recruitment, morale, productivity, and professional development and retention. Brian O'Connell, founding president of Independent Sector, argues persuasively that it is essential not only to improve the compensation policies of individual organizations, but also to elevate this dimension of the entire sector. Everyone involved in the nonprofit world shares an opportunity and an obligation to develop compensation practices that are fully consistent with the challenges and expectations that we have for this sector. A distinctive U.S. contradiction is our tendency to expect extraordinary accomplishments from nonprofits, but to support them so poorly. Nowhere is this contradiction more apparent than in nonprofit compensation policies. We view nonprofits as vital parts of healthy communities, and we applaud their greater ability to address certain challenges; we (finally) expect them to be well managed, but we ask them to do these things while systematically underpaying their employees. The clear, comprehensive picture provided by *Nonprofit Compensation and Benefits Practices* can play a part in addressing this paradox.

In 1990, ARDI completed a cross-sector study of nonprofit salaries and benefits, issuing the study "COMP KEY Effective Compensation: A Key to Non-Profit Success," which has been used widely. More recently, ARDI issued "Innovative Compensation Practices in the Nonprofit Sector." This work extends ARDI's continuing leadership on the topic and reinforces its reputation for analytical rigor and producing practical tools.

January 1998

Robert M. Hollister
Dean of the Graduate School of Arts and Sciences
Research and Professional Studies
Tufts University

Applied Research and Development Institute International, Inc. (ARDI) is dedicated to improving nonprofit management and leadership by making existing resources accessible and creating new resources based on applied research.

Carol L. Barbeito is the founding president of the Applied Research and Development Institute International. She has 25 years of executive management experience. Among her numerous publications are eight on nonprofit compensation, and she holds a doctor of philosophy degree from the University of Denver.

Jack P. Bowman was general manager of the Applied Research and Development Institute International until June 1997. Prior to that he was involved in the small business community. He has a master's degree in business administration from the University of Denver.

Acknowledgments

The Applied Research and Development Institute International, Inc. (ARDI), would like to thank the following individuals and organizations without whose help this project and book would not have been possible.

James E. Rocco, James E. Rocco & Associates—Compensation Consultants. Principal author and researcher of the 1995 ARDI publication *Innovative Compensation Practices in the Nonprofit Sector*, Mr. Rocco also provided input as a reader for this project.

The Advisory Committee for the *Innovative Compensation Practices in the Nonprofit Sector* study gave freely of their expertise and contributed substantially in shaping the study. Their participation is highly valued, and ARDI thanks them. Members include:

Larry Guillot
Executive Director
Center for Management Assistance

George Johnson
Vice President of Human Resources
National Urban League

Jim Moss
Principal
Towers Perrin

Don Robins
Manager, Compensation and Benefits
American Heart Association

Richard Steinberg
Department of Economics
Indiana University/Purdue University at Indianapolis

The ARDI Board of Directors authorized this current project and
provided support and oversight. Their continuing work on behalf of ARDI is invaluable. The directors are:

Elizabeth T. Boris, Ph.D.
Director
Center on Nonprofits and Philanthropy, The Urban Institute

L. Patt Franciosi
Vice President for North America
World Federation for Mental Health
ARDI Board Vice-Chair

Preston Garrison
President
The Garrison Companies
ARDI Board Treasurer

Jennifer Henderson
Director of Training
Center for Community Change

Douglas Kinzley
Vice-Chairman
MGA Communications
ARDI Board Chair

Wilson C. Levis
Senior Research Associate (Retired)
Baruch College

Astrid E. Merget, Ph.D.
Associate Dean and Chair, Department of Public Administration
Maxwell School of Citizenship and Public Affairs, Syracuse
University

Ann Mitchell Sackey
Executive Director
National Council of Nonprofit Associations
ARDI Board Secretary

Cynthia Sadler
Director of External Relations
Civic Education Project

John Palmer Smith, Ph.D.
Executive Director
Mandel Center for Nonprofit Organizations, Case Western
Reserve University

Staff for the Project:

Carol L. Barbeito, Ph.D.
President, ARDI
Coauthor and project director

Jay Bowman
General Manager, ARDI
Coauthor and principal researcher cross-sector study

Julianne Stephens
Administrator, ARDI
Research and editorial assistance

Ann Werner
Director of Programs and Research, ARDI
Editorial assistance

Mia Peters
Secretary, ARDI
Administrative and clerical assistance

Naomi Reich
Intern, ARDI
Research assistance

CHAPTER ONE

Introduction

BACKGROUND

It is difficult to think of anything in the nonprofit sector that generates more discomfort and controversy than a discussion of staff compensation. Great divergence of views and vast misinformation concerning the subject are common. But one reality remains constant: the people in a nonprofit organization are truly the organization's first and preeminent asset.

Nonprofit workers come in two varieties, paid and unpaid. Their resulting relationship comprises one of the unique features of the sector. In a typical nonprofit organization, the volunteer board of directors is a group of unpaid workers that carries out the governing role. They hire a paid executive director to recruit and organize the rest of the workforce. The paid staff, both at the executive level and at other levels, recruit and work to motivate and retain volunteers. Their success in developing a volunteer workforce depends substantially on their ability to match work opportunities to the interests and motivations of the volunteers.

Nonprofit organizations carry in them the heart of our society. They perform the functions that make us civilized: caring for the dying, teaching children, protecting the environment, and releasing beauty. Without them, it is hard to imagine what our world would be like.

Beginning during the 1980s and continuing to date, nonprofit organizations came under increasing pressure not only to "do good," but to do it effectively and efficiently. In light of this trend, nonprofit executives and other managers need to know appropriate management and leadership techniques and how to adapt them to their work environments. They also need to be competent in the unique aspects of managing a nonprofit: fund-raising, volunteer management, and board of directors development. In addition to the preceding, many nonprofits are coping with increased need and demand for both existing services and new services, with greater competition for funds, and with pressure to raise funds from earned-income ventures. Recruitment, motivation, and retention of qualified staff and volunteers have become harder due to increased competition. The resulting work environment is most demanding.

Consequently, nonprofits are aggressively seeking information and assistance to help them effectively administer and compete for human resources. In response to this search, the Technical Assistance Center (TAC) published the first "National Nonprofit Wage and Benefit Survey" (5) in 1988. This was soon followed by a second study, "Compensation in Nonprofit Organizations" (4), sponsored by The Society for Nonprofit Organizations, and another study by Abbott, Langer and Associates resulting in their "Compensation in Nonprofit Organizations" (1) survey. Other studies at national, state, and city/county levels specific to the nonprofit sector also contributed to new understanding of compensation practices.

However, knowing about the practices of the nonprofit sector is not enough because many people are eligible to fill positions in the for-profit and government sectors as well. Therefore, we also need to know how the nonprofit sector's compensation practices compare with the other sectors. Such knowledge is critical if nonprofits are to survive the trends that are creating increased competition for a shrinking pool of talented employees.

To arm the sector with this knowledge, in 1990 ARDI conducted a "Cross-Sector Nonprofit Wage and Benefit Study." The study revealed how nonprofit compensation compared with government and for-profit compensation. It also reported on national workforce, nonprofit, and employment trends and related these to the issue of how the nonprofit sector can recruit and retain quality personnel in the 1990s. The publication resulting from this study was "COMP KEY Effective Compensation: A Key to Non-Profit Success" (2).

ARDI conducted an additional study, which detailed information on innovative compensation practices and provided case studies on how such practices were being implemented by nonprofit organizations. The resulting 1995 publication was "Innovative Compensation Practices in the Nonprofit Sector" (3).

Growing interest and the need for up-to-date cross-sector and innovative compensation information for nonprofit organizations led to the current publication, which includes workforce, employment, and compensation trend analyses, a new cross-sector wage-and-benefit study based upon 1995 data, and updated information on innovative compensation. This book also guides the reader through steps to take to further develop an organization's compensation practices and provides referrals to other resources.

The benefits to a nonprofit organization from well-designed compensation practices are many and have great impact on the success of the organization. Nothing will influence mission accomplishment more than the quality of the people working to achieve it. This, of course, includes the board and unpaid staff, but the focus here is on the paid workers. If the paid staff have the proper qualifications, knowledge, and experience, the organization gains in credibility, productivity, and effectiveness. Each worker is a vital part of the whole, and all positions require careful attention to ensure that compensation practices allow for recruitment and retention of qualified personnel.

UNDERSTANDING THE CONTEXT FOR COMPENSATION PROGRAMS

It is best to look at human resource management within the overall context of all the management functions of an organization. ARDI has worked over the past six years to develop a classification of the field of nonprofit management and leadership that will allow everyone to understand, in an organized system, the functions and subfunctions that comprise the whole field. The title for this classification is "Nonprofit Management and Leadership Taxonomy." The full taxonomy appears in Appendix A.

One of the broad headings in the taxonomy is "human resource management," which covers the management and development of people as a resource. The narrower categories within this broad heading include: administrative systems, compensation, employment and career search, interpersonal, organization, policies, recruitment, volunteer management, general, and other. As you can see, compensation must be viewed in the context of the overall human resource management system, and decisions relating to compensation are affected by and affect other aspects of the system. It is beyond the scope of this book to cover all the other subfunctions, but it will provide considerable information on compensation management in nonprofits and will point out closely related areas.

Later in this book, specifics are provided on how to go about establishing compensation programs. It should be clear from the preceding discussion that this is an important responsibility of both the board and the executive, which has broad ramifications for the organization.

Chapter Two provides you with information that will help you get a quick grasp of overall and nonprofit-sector workforce trends and with an overview of compensation trends and how they relate to trends in compensation in the nonprofit sector. This background provides the setting for more specific research regarding a cross-sector study of wages and benefits, followed by results from the study of innovative compensation in nonprofits.

With the above information in mind, the chapter then provides guidance on how you might proceed to establish or review and update compensation policies and practices in your nonprofit organizations. Information on how to go beyond this book to find other help if you need it is supplied. Also, an extensive bibliography is supplied for further study.

For those of you with considerable knowledge and experience in developing and/or administering compensation policies and practices in nonprofit organizations, this book will give you an opportunity to update your knowledge and to reflect upon future options. Others of you who may be at the initial stage of learning and application can use the chapter on how to obtain additional resources to continue to expand your mastery of the subject.

We sincerely hope that by the end of this book, all of you will be even more committed to excellence in this aspect of the management of your nonprofit agency and will feel informed and empowered to proceed in the development of a fair and competitive compensation program.

REFERENCES

1. Abbott, Langer & Associates, *Compensation in Nonprofit Organizations, 9th Edition* (Crete, IL: Abbott, Langer & Associates, 1996).

2. Carol L. Barbeito, Ph.D., *COMP KEY Effective Compensation: A Key to Non-Profit Success* (Denver, CO: Applied Research and Development Institute International, Inc., 1990).

3. James E. Rocco, *Innovative Compensation Practices in the Nonprofit Sector* (Denver, CO: Applied Research and Development Institute International, Inc., 1995).

4. Society for Nonprofit Organizations, *Compensation in Nonprofit Organizations* (Madison, WI: Society for Nonprofit Organizations, 1989).

5. Technical Assistance Center, *1988 National Nonprofit Wage & Benefits Survey* (Denver, CO: Technical Assistance Center, 1988).

CHAPTER TWO

Workforce, Employment, and Nonprofit Sector Trends

This chapter provides data that will aid your understanding of United States employment trends, including workforce demographics, worker distribution, and changing job requirements. The information provides a context for developing your own workforce strategies and policies. These national trends spotlight an increasingly competitive environment for a declining group of qualified workers, which will be a matter of some concern to nonprofit organizations.

WORKFORCE TRENDS AND DEMOGRAPHICS

According to the Bureau of Labor Statistics "Occupational Out-look Handbook" (2), the labor force is growing and will continue to grow faster than the population. This is driven, at least par-tially, by a growth in the number of women in the workforce. Although many women still occupy lower paying jobs, more women are rapidly moving into professional and technical fields (2). The number of older workers is expanding while the num-ber of younger workers diminishes.

Today, white men comprise a much smaller share of the total number of new entrants into the workforce than do minorities and immigrants, whereas minorities and immigrants make up a larger share of the total population and workforce. Over the next seven years, Hispanic and Asian representation in the workforce is expected to increase at a rate faster than that for African American and white workers. But white workers will still be the vast majority of workers in the year 2005 (2). Persons with disabilities are making inroads into the workforce, with 31.8 per-cent employed compared with 78.6 percent for nondisabled workers (6).

EMPLOYMENT TRENDS

Comparing these workforce trends with employment trends generates concern. A slowdown in overall employment growth is predicted (2). Manufacturing will comprise a much smaller share of the U.S. economy, with a resulting loss of jobs. An ex-ception exists for systems analysts and other computer-related positions, which are showing an increase in growth. Traditional management positions are being compressed, which also results in a subsequent loss of jobs (5). This trend of compressing man-agement has been led by "re-engineering" within the corporate community, and government and nonprofit organizations have undertaken similar strategies.

The number of jobs in the service industry is increasing more rapidly than in other areas, with business, health, and education showing the most growth. The job growth in the health care industry is related to increasing numbers of elderly persons and to increased use of innovative technology for intensive diagnosis and treatment. Personal-service needs are up, but these jobs often have low pay, low job stability, and poor benefits. These jobs also require low training (2). This growth in service-industry jobs may help to partially offset the loss of manufacturing jobs that are traditionally filled by less-educated and less-skilled people and that are being eliminated by expert systems and other forms of artificial intelligence.

Another trend is the increased use of temporary help instead of permanent employees. For employers, use of temporary workers has the advantage of more flexibility and, in many cases, of decreased costs and long-term obligations. Employees may value the flexibility, but this often means they receive lower wages and benefits. Outsourcing of work is also growing (5).

The result of these trends generates concern for underemployment or unemployment for those with less education and fewer skills because the demand for such workers is decreasing in many industry categories. An opposite situation exists for those workers with highly specialized skills and postsecondary education. There will be fewer qualified workers for an increasing number of positions. This trend indicates that greater competition will occur among employers for a shrinking pool of highly educated and skilled workers (2).

There has been a decline in the influence of labor unions, which Jeremy Rifkin (5) tied to a decline in average wages. He stated that "during the 1980s, the hourly wages of 80 percent of the American workforce declined by an average of 4.9 percent." Rifkin also noted that worker benefits declined in this same period. An exception to this decline is an increasing tendency for executive pay to grow out of proportion to other workers (5, 1). Others whose pay is growing at an above-average pace are the new professionals who are highly trained knowledge workers.

Rifkin described this class of workers as a diverse group united by their use of state-of-the-art information technology to identify, process, and solve problems. Some examples he gave of such workers are research scientists, public relations specialists, management consultants, strategic planners, writers, and editors, among others.

NONPROFIT SECTOR TRENDS AND DEMOGRAPHICS

To understand how these trends may impact their organizations, nonprofits need to know where their sector stands in relation to the overall employment picture. Paid employees in the nonprofit sector constitute 10.6 percent of the total workforce in the United States. The number of people employed in the IRS (Internal Revenue Service) nonprofit designations is 9.7 million. Employment in the nonprofit sector has grown at a faster rate than in the business sector over the past seventeen years (4).

Demographic characteristics of the nonprofit sector workforce show it to be largely female. In 1994, women comprised 68.2 percent of paid employees. African American paid employees represented 15 percent and Hispanics 6 percent of the nonprofit workforce. Nonprofit managerial and professional employees are well educated compared to the general workforce, with a high percentage holding advanced degrees. The nonprofit sector provides major employment opportunities for some occupations such as clergy, managers in service organizations, registered nurses, health care managers, and others providing professional services to individuals (4).

The nonprofit sector is under considerable stress. The number of nonprofit organizations as a share of all national entities declined from 1977 to 1992, but it has held steady since then (4). The following trends (7, 8, 3) are considered relevant to this decline and subsequent plateau:

- Cutbacks in government services and government funding for services
- The reduction of income-tax incentives for charitable contributions
- A decline in corporate cash giving
- Increased demand for services
- Higher demand for public accountability
- Greater expectations for managers and directors

Government cutbacks in both grants and contracts, increased service demands without obvious funding sources to pay for them, a decline in corporate cash giving, plus a trend for corporations to tie donations to business strategy have created a highly competitive resource-raising environment. Presumably, at least partially in response to these trends, nonprofits are increasingly turning to earned-income strategies to raise funds. Earned income is the fastest growing source of funds for nonprofits and creates pressure for acquisition of new skills among managers and boards. In reaction to this increased emphasis on enterprise, small business owners are expressing concern over "unfair" competition from nonprofit entities.

On a positive note, there has been a growth in the formation of new foundations. Overall foundation giving and individual giving are up. Corporate in-kind contributions are up, somewhat mitigating the decline in their cash giving (4).

There are indications of increased general awareness of the nonprofit sector and its role in society. Media coverage has increased. The last three U.S. presidents have established well-publicized national task forces to stimulate volunteerism and philanthropy. Organizations such as the Independent Sector have formed at a national level to conduct research on, advocate on behalf of, and create awareness of the nonprofit sector. Also, there are a growing number of colleges offering studies related to the nonprofit sector.

With this background on national workforce, employment, and nonprofit trends, it is now appropriate to focus specifically on compensation trends.

REFERENCES

1. Debra E. Blum, Paul Demko, Susan Gray, and Holly Hall, "Top Dollar for Charities' Top Leaders," *Chronicle of Philanthropy* 8, no. 23 (19 Sept. 1996).

2. Bureau of Labor Statistics, 1996, "Occupational Outlook Handbook," *Bureau of Labor Statistics* (On-line). Available: http://stats.bls.gov/oco/oco2003.htm.

3. Peter Drucker, 1989, "Peter Drucker on the Non-profit Environment," *The Taft Non-profit Executive* 9, no. 3 (November 1989).

4. Virginia Ann Hodgkinson and Murray S. Weitzman, *Nonprofit Almanac 1996–1997: Dimensions of the Independent Sector* (San Francisco: Jossey-Bass Publishers, 1996).

5. Jeremy Rifkin, *The End of Work: The Decline of the Global Labor Force and the Dawn of the Post-Market Era* (New York: G.P. Putnam's Sons, 1995).

6. Janet Simms, "Disabled Making Inroads in the Workplace," *Rocky Mountain News* (November 15, 1995).

7. Taft Group, "A Futuristic Look, Trends in the Nonprofit Sector," *The Taft Non-profit Executive* 8, no. 11 (August 1989).

CHAPTER THREE

Compensation Trends

If nonprofits are to position themselves to recruit, motivate, and retain quality personnel, they need to take into account cross-sector compensation trends (25). Reward systems have three components: economic, social, and psychological. Economic rewards have traditionally been larger in the for-profit sector and are certainly an important consideration. However, social and psychological factors are also powerful motivators that nonprofits may be well positioned to use to increase their competitive advantage. The integration of workforce trends (see Chapter Four), compensation trends, and studies illuminating workforce motivations provide useful information on which to build individual organization policies and strategies.

TRENDS IN CROSS-SECTOR COMPENSATION PRACTICES

Market pricing of jobs has been used extensively by for-profit companies (18). This method of determining compensation helps an organization to ensure that its salary structure is competitive with other businesses. The best companies establish policies calculated to position their compensation competitively. They are concerned not only with attracting the best qualified people to fill positions but also with retaining them. For-profits have documented that the cost of replacing an employee is approximately five to six times the employee's monthly salary (30, 26). Therefore, retaining employees is imperative to keeping training costs at a minimum.

Compensation Strategies

In the for-profit sector, the average merit increases hovered at about 4 percent in 1995 and 1996 (42). Analysts predicted a similar 3.51 percent increase for for-profit organizations in 1997 (16). Merit increases are less popular with employers than they used to be as a form of pay increase. It is believed employees come to see merit increases as an entitlement, and merit levels become intertwined with cost-of-living indexes.

The exception to the flat trend in pay increases is directors' and executives' pay, which increased between two and three times the level of inflation in 1995. A tight market for senior positions drove these higher increases (17). Jeremy Rifkin noted that top executive compensation is greatly outpacing other employee groups through generous incentive pay systems and special benefit programs (34). One example of this is SERPs (Supplemental Employee Retirement Programs) used by large banks to restore benefits to top executives not covered under qualified retirement programs (9).

There is a lack of reporting on gender-difference data in the overall trends. The results of a study on wage-and-benefit trends with gender differences as a focus might well demonstrate differences between males and females for the preceding findings. The Institute of Management Administration (IOMA) reported the following in "Studies Document the Effects of Gender on Compensation": "Regardless of the field, in the end the findings are pretty much the same: even when men and women have the same job title or responsibility and the same amount of experience, they don't make the same pay . . ." (15).

For-profits commonly use a combination of base pay, benefits, perquisites, and incentive pay, not only as recruitment tools but also as managerial controls and as checks on fair compensation practices (19, 20). Recent for-profit trends show perquisites being cut back, except for home-security systems, tax-planning for executive staff, and individual employee financial counseling (5, 44). Trends also show an increase in lump-sum payments, from 29 percent in 1995 to 40 percent in 1996, by the companies reporting in the *Salary Management Planning Survey* published by Towers Perrin (42). The incentive for using lump-sum rewards is to control fixed costs of payroll and to link pay to performance against individual employee goals. The same principle is being applied to work-unit performance. The work unit can be a team, department, division, and so on.

Performance incentives in the form of stock options and bonuses are very popular in for-profit firms. The Institute of Management Administration's Report on Salary Survey related that the majority of employees (62.5 percent) in for-profit firms will be receiving bonuses in 1997, whereas nonprofit employers project offering bonuses to only 31 percent of their employees. These bonuses are being incorporated into compensation plans based upon company performance (26). In for-profit companies, stock options are often used as long-term motivators and are tied to performance of the company.

Nonprofit organizations may believe they are legally prohibited from using supplemental pay systems. This is not the case, although, because there are no shareholders, stocks are not an option. The IRS Counsel Memorandum 38283, Revenue Ruling 8122068 1980, specifically removed prohibitions against the use of profit-sharing incentive pay systems in nonprofit organizations. Charities will not jeopardize their federal tax exemptions if they use some form of incentive system (1). In fact, the use of merit pay, bonuses, and incentive pay in addition to regular pay is on the increase in nonprofit organizations (37, 14).

Another motivational strategy that is becoming more common is *skill-based pay* (24, 26)—people are paid according to the skills they have, not the job they hold. Skill broadening, either vertically or horizontally, is rewarded by pay increases. Both performance-based and skill-based pay require a clear understanding of the methods and their pluses and minuses to make them successful (25, 41). The March-April 1993, *Compensation & Benefits Review* included an article entitled "Who Uses Skill-Based Pay, and Why" (27). The authors, Edward E. Lawler III, Lei Chang, and Gerald E. Ledford Jr., conducted a study of employee-involvement practices, with usable data from 313 Fortune 1000 firms. The article described how skill-based pay is a compensation option available to both for-profit and nonprofit employers. Employees can add to their income with skill-based pay by renewing, updating, and broadening their skills, knowledge, and useful capabilities. Employees' pay increases are based upon their increasing contribution to the organization, rather than on entitlements, such as length of service or cost of living. Skill-based pay may be an advantageous option for companies facing intensive competitive pressure, downsizing, or a desire to encourage employee involvement. The authors' research indicated manufacturing firms were more likely than service firms to adopt skill-based pay programs. The research results found that skill-based pay was associated with a variety of other innovative pay practices related to employee involvement, such as profit sharing, all-salaried pay systems, and team incentives. Of the 313 companies surveyed, 185, or 59 percent, that used skill-based pay also used gainsharing (27).

Benefits

Benefits are an important part of the compensation package and are becoming more flexible and portable. Most full-time workers are covered by diverse benefits, with the most commonly offered being health benefits, paid vacation, paid holidays, and employer-provided life insurance. The next most commonly offered are paid sick leave and retirement plans. Health benefits are moving to nontraditional forms such as health maintenance organizations or other managed care programs. Increasingly, employees are being asked to contribute to their health care plans and costs (6).

Improving productivity, motivating employees, and linking pay to performance pose ongoing challenges for many organizations. Employers' efforts to address these issues often encompass a wide range of strategies, including reexamination of their current compensation programs and the development and implementation of innovative compensation plans. Leading contributors in the trend toward innovative compensation practices include the following:

- Increased competition for staff and resources among the growing number of nonprofits and between certain types of charities and the private sector
- Higher demands for accountability from constituents, boards, and the general public
- The need for more cost controls
- Greater emphasis on pay-for-performance and less on pay-as-entitlement
- Better linkage of compensation plans to overall organizational goals (37).

In an effort to determine prevalence and characteristics of innovative pay plans, The Bureau of National Affairs (BNA) conducted a survey among members of its Personnel Policies Forum in 1989, with a follow-up survey in 1991 (7). It should be noted that 75 percent of the participants are for-profit organizations. Exhibit 3.1 indicates the prevalence of innovative compensation programs, based on all 191 companies in the survey and 98 large companies (1,000 or more employees).

Innovative compensation plans have grown over the past several years in response to new working arrangements and expectations of both employees and employers. On March 17, 1993, Steven E. Gross and Lee McCullough, vice Presidents of the Hay Group, made a speech entitled "Alternative Rewards: Do They Work?" to the New York Compensation Association. Gross and McCullough described the employee and employer expectations of the new work arrangement in for-profit organizations as follows (32):

Employee Expectations	*Employer Expectations*
Effective leadership	Value-added contribution
Participation in decisions	Responsiveness to environment
Balanced risk/reward	Quality/customer focus
Opportunity for advancement	Commitment to work unit
Stimulating job content	Pay plans linked to business results

Exhibit 3.1   Prevalence of Innovative Compensation Plans

Type of Company	All	Large
No. of Companies	191	98
Organizations with one or more innovative compensation plans	54%	63%
Spot bonuses	26%	31%
Individual incentives	25%	29%
Profit sharing	13%	17%
Group incentives	11%	12%
Gain sharing	2%	3%
Other	1%	—

Source: Excerpted from *Non-Traditional Incentive Pay Programs*, Personnel Policies Forum Survey No. 148, Table 1. p. 2 (May 1991). Copyright 1991 by The Bureau of National Affairs, Inc. (800-372-1033) (7).

Jim Braham, in an article entitled "A Rewarding Place to Work," discussed several methods of rewarding employees, both extrinsically and intrinsically, used by for-profit companies. Intrinsic rewards, such as recognition and the opportunity to grow, learn, and advance, may motive people quite effectively. Notwithstanding, there should be enough extrinsic rewards (i.e., cash) available before the intrinsic rewards can become most effective. Edward Lawler, Ph.D., an expert on employee involvement, was quoted in this same article as saying he believes "it's a false dichotomy to separate money and recognition programs." To him, "money *is* a form of recognition. The issue, for organizational effectiveness, is to integrate the two so they complement each other and work together" (4).

Although some cash rewards do work, Bob Filipczak, staff editor of *Training* magazine, contended that "the best rewards are noncash" (12). He claimed that cash rewards are spent like a salary, and as a result they get taken for granted. Generally, employees are more comfortable talking about noncash rewards, rather than cash rewards. A noncash reward may remind the employee of the company's appreciation.

In an article entitled "Morale Coupons," Tom Dunaway described how a company in Virginia issues its employees a book of recognition coupons. The company encourages employees to give their fellow employees one or more coupons when an employee is observed doing something that contributes to company goals. Employees take part in determining what awards will be available. The coupons may be redeemed for awards such as merchandise or restaurant gift certificates, car wash certificates, or postage stamps. Employee morale has improved as a result of this program. It has also increased employees' understanding of how their contributions impact the company's goals (10).

According to Charles M. Cumming, Senior Compensation Consultant at William M. Mercer, Incorporated, there *are* incentives that motivate employees, as long as they are properly designed. Team or group incentives are effective because they can acknowledge the participants' need to see the results of their collective success. In the traditional for-profit organization, emphasis is on individual achievement, rather than on the team. Employees may be asked to accomplish tasks that do not match the team goal. This approach leaves employees struggling to find intrinsic value or satisfaction in performing work that may mean little or nothing to someone else (8).

Progressive, leading companies are creating ways to balance both the company's and the employees' needs. Companies are interested in learning how to improve quality, productivity, competitiveness, and profits. Assigning a team of workers with the responsibility for specific task outcomes is one example of creating this balance. When employees perceive that their efforts and accomplishments create value, and they participate in incentive programs designed to reinforce these perceptions, the incentives will tend to enhance employees' level of intrinsic satisfaction (8).

Incentive programs in nonprofit organizations often focus on rewarding top executives and managers because these employees are critical to the organization's success. To attract, retain, and motivate such talent, an innovative compensation-and-benefits package, based on a pay-for-performance philosophy, has been reported as effective by some nonprofits that have instituted such plans (37).

A typical innovative compensation package used by nonprofit organizations includes the following elements (35):

- Competitive salary
- Annual incentives
- Supplemental benefits
- Perquisites
- Employment contracts

Exhibit 3.2 lists the major elements of executive compensation (for all sectors), as defined in Ernst and Young's 1990 *National Survey of Executive Compensation*, and the impact each element has on overall compensation objectives. Base salary and perquisites

Exhibit 3.2   Impact of Compensation Elements on Overall Objectives

Element	Attraction	Retention	Motivation
Base salary	High	High	Low/medium
Annual incentives	Medium	Medium	High
Long-term incentives	Medium	Medium	High
Benefits	Medium	High	Low
Perquisites	High	Medium	Low

Source: National Survey of Executive Compensation, 4th edition, Ernst & Young, 1990 (11).

(for example automobiles, club memberships, and first-class travel) have the greatest effect on attracting new executives into the organization. Base salary and benefits have the greatest effect on retaining executives for the long term. Annual and long-term incentives have the greatest effect on motivating executives to higher levels of performance.

Exhibit 3.3 indicates the frequency of common executive compensation practices in nonprofits, as reported in several surveys (35).

Other trends include more fluid job descriptions and more flexible work schedules. Working at home and part-time jobs are increasing. Wellness programs, corporate involvement in social agendas, elder care, child care, and adoption services are all being utilized in benefit programs to varying degrees. For-profits are working to counteract the trend of greater competition for well-educated, experienced employees by developing their own employees. Greater emphasis is being placed on developing in-house training programs. Employees also are increasingly viewed as

Exhibit 3.3   Frequency of Use by Nonprofits of Compensation Elements

Element	Frequency
Employment contracts	48%
Supplemental life insurance plans	35%
Supplemental medical plans	26%
Annual incentive plans	23%
Supplemental retirement plans	23%
Supplemental disability plans	21%

Source: Rocco, "How to Attract the Brightest People," Nonprofit World, May/June 1992 (35).

company assets. In response to changes in the composition of the workforce, businesses increasingly have to manage cultural diversity (2), and therefore business plans are integrating human resource planning (45).

MOTIVATING EMPLOYEES

To effectively motivate employees, it is important to review studies on different segments of the workforce. The American Management Association's (AMA) report on age-related motivations provides helpful information (21). Younger workers want performance-based pay, job enlargement, job enrichment, and task-related projects. Other studies on younger workers reinforce the AMA findings (3). Younger workers desire immediate involvement in the essential work of the company and rapid skill and career development. Middle-aged and older workers are most interested in job security, health care, and pension programs.

The AMA studied female workers separately. In 1990, the AMA published a report on different segments of the workforce, entitled *Human Resources Strategic Mandates for the 1990s* (21). The report indicated that women valued family medical leaves, child care, pooled sick time, flextime, summer work hours, four-day weeks, split days, and job sharing. These findings suggest that women continue to provide most child and/or elder care needs.

HOW CROSS-SECTOR COMPENSATION PRACTICES ARE AFFECTING THE NONPROFIT SECTOR

Focusing now on the nonprofit sector, we see that in spite of comparatively low salaries and benefits, employment in the sector is up. The number of graduate programs in nonprofit management is slowly growing—a recent study currently underway by Seton Hall University has identified over seventy nonprofit-management-specific, higher education programs. ACCESS, a nonprofit job-matching service, reports a growing interest in crossover from for-profits to nonprofits, with the most successful crossover positions in finance, computers, sales, and public relations (28, 29).

Brian O'Connell, retired founding president of Independent Sector, identified four problems of compensation in nonprofit organizations. First, some salaries and other compensation are flagrantly high. He noted that we must be intolerant of such excess to preserve the integrity of the sector. The second problem is that some may *perceive* compensation to be too high out of lack of understanding of the demands of the jobs. To address this concern, O'Connell called for boards of directors to be involved in setting compensation and defending their decisions once it is set. The third problem comes from a mistaken belief that salaries are an overhead cost. Indeed, salaries comprise most of the costs of services that are directly related to the mission of the organization. Because this is the case, O'Connell recommended adopting functional accounting practices so nonprofits can demonstrate what they spend on services versus management and fund-raising. Finally, he noted most importantly that the vast majority of nonprofit workers are compensated at such a low level that it threatens the development and maintenance of essential services. He called for careful attention to building compensation programs that will make it possible for nonprofits to recruit and retain qualified staff in order to ensure that the service needs of our communities can be well met (33).

Our cross-sector wage-and-benefit study (Chapter Six) specifically supports O'Connell's fourth point. Nonprofit salaries are indeed low when compared to other sectors. In fact, salary levels are lowest in the nonprofit sector for five of the eight benchmark positions that ARDI (Applied Research and Development Institute) used in the study: executive director, deputy director, department director, office manager, and secretary. Furthermore, salary-level disparity between sectors increases as you move from clerical to managerial positions. The gap between the nonprofit and the for-profit sectors for overall median salaries at the managerial/professional level is typically 100 percent and in extreme cases as high as 400 percent. The gap at the technical/clerical level is a much smaller 20 percent.

An article called "Labor Economics and the Nonprofit Sector: A Literature Review" by Richard Steinberg, published in the summer of 1990 in the *Nonprofit and Voluntary Sector Quarterly* (39), noted some interesting statistics comparing workers in the nonprofit and the for-profit sectors. Steinberg cited surveys that indicated "the typical nonprofit worker earns 33 percent less than the typical for-profit worker, although nonprofit workers are both more educated and more likely to work in a professional occupation. Despite this lower pay, nonprofit workers claim a greater level of job satisfaction, reporting that their jobs provide variety, autonomy, and flexibility. Nonprofits are less likely to use incentive clauses in worker contracts."

In recent years, a number of nonprofits have radically changed the way they pay their top executives. Many nonprofits have moved from relying exclusively on fixed salaries to advocating variable pay as a part of their total cash compensation program. A survey conducted by the consulting firm Towers Perrin indicated that 42 percent of the approximately 300 nonprofits surveyed used variable cash compensation programs in 1994, up from 10 percent in 1982 (43). All types of organizations use variable pay programs, although they are more common among trade associations and professional societies than human services and cultural arts groups. Incentive awards in nonprofits ranged from 6 to 13 percent of total compensation (salary plus incentives). Depending on managerial levels, the comparable figure in the private sector ranged from 20 to 50 percent (36).

There are many reasons that nonprofit organizations, particularly larger nonprofits, are starting to move away from traditional entitlement pay programs, which emphasize base salary, to variable compensation programs, which focus on performance. One of the reasons for this strategic change is the commitment of organizations to use money as a reward for superior performance, starting at the Chief Executive Officer (CEO) level. There is also a cost-control feature that is attractive to nonprofits. Variable compensation can replace a portion of fixed-pay costs (salary) with a cost that varies with performance (pay at risk) (38).

In his article "Financial Incentives for Nonprofits," Jay Wein stated that, "in general, people who are attracted to nonprofits are more likely to be driven by altruistic motives and less by money than those who gravitate to for-profit settings" (45). In the current marketplace, nonprofits are competing for talented people who may be motivated by a mixture of financial need as well as a sense of mission. This issue should be carefully addressed by nonprofit organizations when designing innovative pay plans.

In her article "Charities' Bonus Debate," Holly Hall stated that incentives were considered as a nonrecurring expense, which improved employee morale. In periods of economic uncertainty, a few nonprofits considered incentives/bonuses as a means to avoid providing salary increases that would permanently increase their payroll and benefits costs (13).

Nonprofits that are considering innovative compensation plans should be aware of the potential debate surrounding issues related to such plans. Incentive compensation plans were long considered controversial for nonprofits because they were seen by some as taking away from the mission and the goals of nonprofits. Donors and the general public might not be comfortable with potential plan awards being paid from contributions.

One of the key concerns with the appropriateness of incentives is whether bonuses should be paid to fund-raisers. Some fund-raisers view bonuses along the same lines as a commission. Nonprofit organizations are concerned about donors' potential reactions. If incentive-pay programs were implemented for fund-raisers, how would donors react to a portion of their contributions being used in this way? Still others think fund-raisers would be encouraged by incentive programs to step up their efforts, possibly resulting in larger contributions to the organization (13).

Dennis Young, in his *Performance and Reward in Nonprofit Organizations: Evaluation, Compensation, and Personnel Incentives* working paper, reported that leaders in social service organizations were reluctant to tie compensation of fund-raisers to performance because "fund-raising success depends heavily on . . . economic conditions over which the fund-raiser has no control. Thus, the fund-raiser should not be rewarded for banner years, nor penalized for bad years." Success at meeting fund-raising goals depends partly on luck, and it is hard to determine the effect of the employee (46).

However, it is Rocco's (37) opinion that although economic conditions can have a significant effect on funds raised, the efforts of the fund-raiser should not be undervalued. Success in fundraising is contingent upon and affected by circumstances. The ability of the employee and the organizations to creatively meet these challenges is one rationale for the desirability of innovative compensation plans. A well-designed and flexible plan should take such considerations into account in the determination of potential plan awards.

According to Jay Wein, president, Wein Associates, the issue regarding incentives is "*not* should we (nonprofits) *use* them, but *how should* we (nonprofits) use them." In the current competitive environment, organizations in both the for-profit and the nonprofit sectors are faced with two key challenges—to increase revenues and to contain costs. Nonprofit executives are confronted with a third key challenge—finding new fund-raising sources. Financial incentive awards have resulted in better executive performance in for-profit organizations. In a nonprofit organizations, the overall financial performance could be considered as a key performance criterion in an incentive plan, and the *quality of service* provided may be just as important (45).

Measuring performance is difficult for nonprofits that define *success* not primarily in financial terms, but in terms of mission accomplishment. This issue can be resolved by using "output-based incentive(s)" rather than profitability measures. Another possibility is to use "adjusted profits," which base the incentive plan on cost reduction within the organization (40).

In order to minimize the potential disadvantages of innovative compensation plans, Richard Steinberg suggested nonprofits tie their incentive programs to indicators that best protect the charitable mission of the organization. It is important to incorporate long-term goals into the incentive plan so that managers will not try to take advantage of the plan and then move on to another organization (40).

A nonprofit organization could potentially risk losing its tax-exempt status or incurring other penalties if it implements a poorly designed and administered compensation plan. For example, if the CEO of an organization develops a compensation plan and has direct influence over the plan elements as it affects the CEO's compensation, then this situation could be considered inurement if the compensation he or she receives is viewed to be excessive. A new law, often referred to as the "intermediate sanction," was signed into effect in July 1996; it strengthens this concern, especially as it relates to the role of the board of directors in compensation programs (31, 22).

There are also potential employee relations issues related to innovative compensation plans. For example, in financially troubled nonprofits, paying small bonuses may be perceived by employees as a way to avoid paying annual base salary increases; additionally, employees who are not participants in an innovative compensation plan may react negatively to the plan.

Nonprofit organizations need to pay attention to the trends of increasing competition for a skilled and educated workforce and decreasing use of traditional pay methods in an effort to both cut costs and retain employees and also the nonprofit sector's poor positioning in terms of competitive compensation levels. Chapters Four and Five provide research data that provides specific information on cross-sector comparisons for traditional wages and benefits and nonprofit experiences in utilizing innovative compensation practices.

REFERENCES

1. Elliott I. Alvarado, 1996, "The Validity of Supplemental Pay Systems in Nonprofit Organizations," *Nonprofit Management and Leadership* 6, no. 3, (Spring).

2. Earl W. Anthes and Jerry Cronin, eds., *Personnel Matters in the Nonprofit Organization* (Madison, WI: Society for Nonprofit Organizations, 1996).

3. Janice Y. Benjamin and Marcia A. Manter, "How to Hold Onto First Careerists," *Personnel Administrator* (September 1989).

4. Jim Braham, "A Rewarding Place to Work," *Industry Week* (September 1989).

5. Lynn Brenner, "Crossing the Line," *CFO: The Magazine for Senior Financial Executives* 12 (October 1996).

6. Bureau of Labor Statistics, 1996, "Bureau of Labor Statistics Reports on Employee Benefits in Small Private Industry Establishments, 1994," *Bureau of Labor Statistics* (On-line). Available: http://www.stats.bls.gov/news.release/ebs.toc.htm.

7. Bureau of National Affairs, 1991, "Non-Traditional Incentive Pay Programs," *Personnel Policies Forum Survey*, no. 148 (May 1991).

8. Charles M. Cumming, "Incentives That Really Do Motivate," *Compensation & Benefits Review* (May-June 1994).

9. Denise Duclaux, "Beyond Paychecks," *ABA Banking Journal* 88 (October 1996).

10. Tom Dunaway, "Morale Coupons," *Training & Development* (May 1992).

11. Ernst & Young LLP, *National Survey of Executive Compensation, 4th Edition* (New York: Ernst & Young, 1990).

12. Bob Filipczak, "Why No One Likes Your Incentive Program," *Training* (August 1993).

13. Holly Hall, "Charities' Bonus Debate," *Chronicle of Philanthropy* (July 1993).

14. Robert D. Herman, *The Jossey-Bass Handbook of Nonprofit Leadership and Management* (San Francisco: Jossey-Bass Publishers, 1994).

15. Institute of Management and Administration (IOMA), 1996, "Effects of Gender on Compensation," *IOMA's Report on Salary Surveys*, IOMA (On-line). Available: http://www.ioma.com/ioma/rss/index.html.

16. Institute of Management and Administration (IOMA), 1996, "Survey Offers Early Estimates of 1997 Merit Pay Increases," *IOMA's Report on Salary Surveys*, IOMA, (On-line). Available: http://www.ioma.com/ioma/rss/index.html.

17. Internal Revenue Service, 1996, "Where to Pitch Your Managers' Pay," *IRS Employment Review*, no. 612 (July 1996).
18. Jill Kanin-Lovers, "Market Pricing," *Journal of Compensation and Benefits* (March/April 1988).
19. Jill Kanin-Lovers, "Salary Structure Design Can Be a Multipurpose Tool," *Journal of Compensation and Benefits* (May/June 1987).
20. Jill Kanin-Lovers, "Total Compensation Analysis: A Broad Perspective," *Journal of Compensation and Benefits* (January/February 1989).
21. Kenneth A. Kovach and John A. Pearce II, *Human Resources Strategic Mandates for the 1990s*, American Management Association, 1990.
22. Daniel L. Kurtz, "Fixing Nonprofit Executive Compensation," *VCG Boardmember's FORUM* (New York: Volunteer Consulting Group, 1996).
23. Steven Langer, "Who's Being Paid What—And Why?," *Nonprofit World* 8, no. 6 (November/December 1990).
24. Edward E. Lawler III, *Merit Pay: An Obsolete Policy* (Berkeley, CA: School of Business Administration, University of Southern California).
25. Edward E. Lawler III, *Pay for Performance: A Motivational Analysis* (Berkeley, CA: School of Business Administration, University of Southern California).
26. Edward E. Lawler III, *The Design of Effective Reward Systems* (Berkeley, CA: School of Business Administration, University of Southern California).
27. Edward E. Lawler, Lei Chang, and Gerald Ledford, "Who Uses Skill-Based Pay, and Why," *Compensation & Benefits Review* (March/April 1993).
28. Tony Lee, "Jobs Abound in the Growing Nonprofit Sector," *National Business Employment Weekly* (17 December 1989).
29. Tony Lee, "Non-profits Ready to Compete for Corporate Executives," *National Business Employment Weekly* (December 1988).
30. Massachusetts Municipal Personnel Association, *Municipal Salary Survey Benchmark Jobs 1989–1990*, Massachusetts Municipal Personnel Association, 1989.
31. John Murawsk, "Law Penalizing Lavish Nonprofit Salaries Causes Uncertainty," *Chronicle of Philanthropy* 8, no. 23 (19 Sept. 1996).
32. New York Compensation Association, "Alternative Rewards: Do

They Work?," *Workforce Compensation*, New York Compensation Association, 1993.

33. Brian O'Connell, "Salaries in Nonprofit Organizations," *Nonprofit World* 10 (July/August, 1991).

34. Jeremy Rifkin, *The End of Work: The Decline of the Global Labor Force and the Dawn of the Post-Market Era* (New York: G.P. Putnam's Sons, 1995).

35. James E. Rocco, "How to Attract the Brightest People," *Nonprofit World* (May/June, 1992).

36. James E. Rocco, "Incentive Plans Help Control Salary Costs," *The Nonprofit Times* (May 1993).

37. James E. Rocco, *Innovative Compensation Practices in the Nonprofit Sector* (Denver, CO: Applied Research and Development Institute International, 1995).

38. James E. Rocco, "Making Incentive Plans Work for Nonprofits," *Nonprofit World* (July/August 1991).

39. Richard Steinberg, "Labor Economics and the Nonprofit Sector: A Literature Review," *Nonprofit and Voluntary Sector Quarterly* 19, no. 2 (Summer 1990).

40. Richard Steinberg, "Profits and Incentive Compensation in Nonprofit Firms," *Nonprofit Management Leadership* 1, no. 2 (Winter 1990).

41. Gerald E. Tedford Jr., *The Effectiveness of Skill-Based Pay Systems* (Los Angeles: Center for Effective Organizations, University of Southern California).

42. Towers Perrin, *1997 Salary Management Planning Survey, Summary Report* (Rosslyn, VA: Towers Perrin, 1996).

43. Towers Perrin, *1994 Management Compensation Report, Not-for-Profit Organizations* (Rosslyn, VA: Towers Perrin, 1994).

44. TPF & C, "The Power of Knowledge," *Salary Management*, issue 113 (1989).

45. Jay R. Wein, "Financial Incentives for Non-Profits," *Fund Raising Management* (September 1989).

46. Dennis Young, *Performance and Reward in Nonprofit Organizations: Evaluation, Compensation, and Personnel Incentives*, Yale University—Program on Nonprofit Organizations, Working Paper No. 79, 1984.

CHAPTER FOUR

Cross-Sector Study of Wages and Benefits

METHODOLOGY OF CROSS-SECTOR WAGE-AND-BENEFIT STUDY

The purpose of this study is to determine what comparisons can be made between the wage-and-benefit practices used by the non-profit, the for-profit, and the government sectors of the United States. Also of interest are the existing differences and similarities in how each sector conducts wage-and-benefit surveys. The information derived from studying these issues, in the context of national workforce, nonprofit, and employment trends, will assist nonprofit organizations in establishing compensation policies and practices that will contribute to successful recruitment and retention of qualified personnel.

Common Benchmark Positions

When comparing wage-and-benefit data across sectors, it is necessary to identify common benchmark positions on which to base the comparisons. Other factors, such as the dollar volume managed by the organization and geographic location, are also important to consider when making comparisons. In the cross-sector comparison study that ARDI published in 1990, eight benchmark positions were used. A panel of nonprofit executives convened by the Technical Assistance Center (TAC) developed the positions and their descriptions for use in its "1989 National Non-profit Wage and Benefit Survey" (4). TAC's survey included fourteen benchmark positions commonly found in nonprofit organizations, and ARDI found that eight of these fourteen positions were common to all sectors or could be used as a standard or point of reference when making comparisons across sectors. The eight benchmark positions have been used again in this study. They are:

- Executive director
- Deputy director
- Department director
- Controller
- Office manager
- Bookkeeper
- Secretary
- Clerk-typist

Six positions from TAC's list were not included. The positions of director of development and volunteer coordinator are commonly found only in the nonprofit sector. The position descriptions for branch director, program specialist, and technician varied widely from sector to sector. The position of maintenance worker, although common to all sectors, was also eliminated because it did not fall in the professional or clerical categories under consideration in this study.

Comparisons between the federal government and the other sectors were difficult, especially at the executive level positions (executive director, deputy director, and department director). The federal government maintains two pay systems at the executive level that could have been used in this study—the Senior Executive Service (SES) and the Executive Schedule. SES position descriptions are not compiled in any one place, and the federal government does not have clearcut standards for establishing them. SES positions vary by location and agency. Therefore, after extensive conversation with the Office of Personnel Management, ARDI decided to use the Title V Executive Level positions and salary scales for this study (see the individual position analyses for sample position titles for all sectors). The Executive Level positions and salary scales are clearly and consistently defined in federal code and apply across agencies and locations. Therefore, these positions are best suited for a cross-sector comparison.

Other Comparison Factors

In addition to the position comparisons, ARDI searched for data that would allow for special comparisons of compensation by region, budget size (or dollar volume managed), and employee gender. These factors are reported in several of the nonprofit surveys found, but the amount and presentation of this information varied widely by sector. Thus, detailed comparison of these factors across sectors is difficult, and this study highlights budget and gender issues only within the nonprofit sector.

In all three sectors, dollar-volume managed was a major factor relating to compensation for executive, managerial, and professional staff. The relevant dollar-volume measures reflect the different characteristics of the sectors—budget size for nonprofits, for-profit sales volume, and authorized expenditures for government. Data on smaller for-profit organizations is difficult to find, and this factor must be taken into account when comparing salaries across the sectors. The nonprofit surveys typically included data from organizations ranging in budget size from $100,000 per year to $5,000,000 and above, whereas the for-profit surveys divided their data into sales volume of more than or less than $100 million.

Survey Data Used in This Study

Eight sources of survey data from the nonprofit sectors were utilized in the study of salaries, four of which were national in scope. The other four sources included data on a regional basis. The nonprofit-sector data excludes professional societies and trade associations and primarily covers the IRS 501(c)(3) category. The sources were:

- *1995 Nonprofit Salary and Benefits Survey of the Greater Kansas City Area*, published by the Center for Management Assistance (8)
- *1995 Survey of New York Metropolitan Area Not-for-Profit Organizations, Compensation and Benefits*, published by Ernst & Young LLP (13)
- *1996 Management Compensation Report, Not-for-Profit Organizations*, published by Towers Perrin (27)
- *1996 Wage & Benefit Survey of Northern California Nonprofit Organizations*, published by The Management Center (18)
- *Compensation in Nonprofit Organizations, 9th Edition*, published by Abbott, Langer & Associates (1)
- *Compensation of Chief Executive Officers in Nonprofit Organizations, 9th Edition*, published by Abbott, Langer & Associates (2)
- *Delaware Nonprofit Wage & Benefit Survey, 1996 Edition*, published by Delaware Association of Nonprofit Agencies (12)

- *Salaries and Benefits in Youth Development Agencies 1996*, published by The National Collaboration for Youth, National Assembly of National Voluntary Health and Social Welfare Organizations (20)

Five sources were utilized from the for-profit sector, they are:

- *1995/1996, Top Management Report*, published by ECS, a Wyatt Data Services Company (14)
- *1996 Survey of Exempt Compensation*, published by Business & Legal Reports, Inc. (5)
- *Compensation Survey of Management Positions in High Technology Companies*, published by Towers Perrin (26)
- "Occupational Compensation Survey, National Summary, 1994," published in 1996 by the U.S. Department of Labor (28)
- "What the Rest of Us Make," data from a national survey conducted in 1996 by William M. Mercer, Inc., for the American Electronics Association (35)

The government sector is divided into three segments: federal, state, and local (city/county).

- Federal data was obtained from the General (15) and Executive Level Pay Scales (analysis from CD-ROM) (4) and the Federal Almanac (17).
- State data was obtained from the Bureau of Labor Statistics (4), the National Association of State Personnel Executives (19), and three state level surveys: California (7), Nebraska (21), and Oklahoma (22).
- The local information is also derived in part from the Bureau of Labor Statistics (4), as well as from five state surveys of local municipalities: Colorado, Texas (25), Pennsylvania (23), Washington, and Florida (16).

In the study of benefits, in addition to relevant data from the surveys cited, the following sources were analyzed:

"Employee Benefits in Small Private Establishments, 1994," published in 1995 by the U.S. Department of Labor (32).

"Employee Benefits in Medium and Large Private Establishments, 1993," published in 1994 by the U.S. Department of Labor (31).

"Employee Benefits in State and Local Governments, 1994," published in 1996 by the U.S. Department of Labor (34).

How the Data Was Analyzed

Eight benchmark-position spreadsheets, with budget-size categories, were created for each of the sectors. Median salary data from nonprofit, for-profit, and federal, state, and local government surveys was entered in the spreadsheets to create sector composites for the eight positions. Each benchmark position is given its own section in this study. The position sections include expanded information on nonprofit salaries including average, median, and 25th and 75th percentile salaries by budget size. Overall average and median salaries and a gender-specific breakout are also provided for the nonprofit sector. Sector comparison data also includes average- and median-salary information but does not include extensive budget size or gender comparisons. Following are definitions for terms found throughout the study:

Salary: The base annual salary, excluding bonuses and other short-term incentives.

25th percentile: The level *below* which 25 percent of the sample falls, or the level *above* which 75 percent of the sample falls.

Median: The middle number in a series, or the level below which 50 percent of the sample falls, i.e., the 50th percentile.

75th percentile: The level *below* which 75 percent of the sample falls, or the level *above* which 25 percent of the sample falls.

Average: The sum of all salary data divided by the number of salaries entered.

Average salary data can be misleading if some of the salaries in a given sample are disproportionately high or low. Therefore, ARDI included both median- and average-salary data.

RESULTS—CROSS-SECTOR SALARY ANALYSIS AND COMPARISONS

This section presents salary data for each benchmark position in summary form across the sectors and individually by position.

Cross-Sector Comparison Summary

Key Findings

- Overall, salary levels are lowest in the nonprofit sector for five of the eight benchmark positions: executive director, deputy director, department director, office manager, and secretary.

- The nonprofit sector paid the second lowest salaries for the remaining three positions: controller, bookkeeper, and clerk-typist.

- The sector salary rankings are identical to those found in the 1990 cross-sector study conducted by ARDI.

- Salary levels have increased in all of the sectors since ARDI conducted its first cross-sector compensation analysis in 1990 (based on data from 1989).

- Salaries in the nonprofit sector have increased approximately 25 percent in the seven years since the 1989 data was gathered, or at a rate of 3.75 percent per year. This percentage varies little between the managerial/professional and the technical/clerical levels—27 and 24 percent respectively.

- Overall, women's salaries are 16 percent less than their male counterparts in the nonprofit sector. The disparity is far greater at the managerial/professional level where women's salaries are 28 percent less than men's. The difference at the technical/clerical level is a much smaller 5 percent.

- Salary-level disparity between the sectors increases as you move from clerical to managerial positions. The gap between the nonprofit and the for-profit sectors for overall median salaries at the managerial/professional level is sometimes as high as 400 percent. The gap at the technical/clerical level is a much smaller 20 percent.

- Regional salary-level differences exist in the nonprofit sector (see Exhibit 4.1). Regional data for all of the sectors was hard to obtain, making sector comparisons difficult.

Cross-Sector Comparison Summary Chart, by Position

Exhibit 4.2 shows the median-salary levels for the eight benchmark positions by sector. The for-profit sector column includes median-salary levels for organizations with less than 100 million in sales (<$100M) and more than $100 million in sales (>$100M).

Exhibit 4.1   Regional Salary Level Differences

Region	Executive Director Median Salary	% above (or below) national median salary of $60,000
Northeast (CT, MA, ME, NH, NJ, NY, PA, RI, VT)	$69,000	15%
South (AL, DC, DE, FL, GA, KY, MD, MS, NC, PR, SC, TN, VA, WV)	$53,000	(13)%
Midwest (IL, IN, MI, OH, WI)	$60,000	—
North Central (IA, KS, MN, MO, ND, NE, SD)	$57,000	(5)%
Southwest (AR, LA, OK, TX)	$65,000	8%
Mountain (AZ, CO, ID, MT, NM, NV, UT, WY)	$56,000	(7)%
Pacific (AK, CA, GU, HI, OR, WA)	$68,393	14%

Source: Based on data from *Compensation of Chief Executive Officers in Nonprofit Organizations, 9th Edition,* Abbott, Langer & Associates, 1996 (2).

Exhibit 4.2   Median Salary Levels for Eight Benchmark Positions

	Nonprofit	For-profit	Federal	State	Local (City/County)
Executive Director	$57,320	$187,265 (<$100M) $336,434 (>$100M)	$148,400	$76,554	$73,332
Deputy Director	$46,025	$157,827 (<$100M) $247,160 (>$100M)	$133,600	$67,740	$61,039
Department Director	$33,130	$85,950 (<$100M) $91,663 (>$100M)	$123,100	$40,055	$53,208
Controller	$40,032	$61,818 (<$100M) $93,800 (>$100M)	$58,838	$51,674	$38,507
Bookkeeper	$22,000	$23,610 (<$100M)	$22,518	$21,133	$23,160
Office manager	$25,740	$39,550 (<$100M)	$30,892	$28,164	$29,553
Secretary	$18,047	$22,953 (<$100M)	$22,518	$21,067	$21,576
Clerk-typist	$15,946	$18,856 (<$100M)	$17,928	$15,576	$18,528

Managerial/Professional Comparison

Exhibit 4.3 shows the managerial/professional positions as a group. The comparison shows an increasing disparity between the sectors as the positions move up to the executive level.

Technical/Clerical Comparison

Exhibit 4.4 shows the technical/clerical positions as a group. The comparison shows less variation for all positions than found in

Exhibit 4.3   Managerial/Professional Comparisons

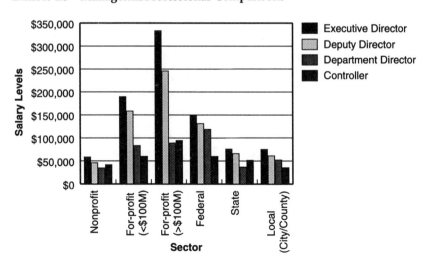

Exhibit 4.4   Technical/Clerical Comparison

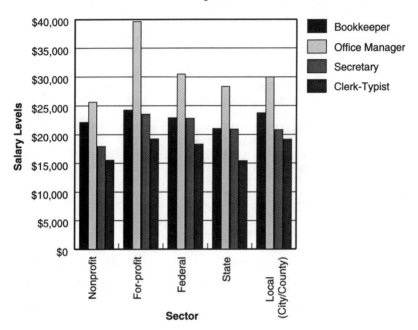

the managerial/professional chart, indicating a lower disparity between the sectors for these positions.

Gender Comparison in the Nonprofit Sector

As ARDI sought input on the design of this study, salary comparisons by gender were often mentioned as a key variable to include. Salary data with gender analysis proved difficult to obtain. Only two of the nonprofit surveys included information on gender (Kansas City and Northern California). A third study (Delaware) analyzed gender-salary comparisons for the executive director position only. The available data is shown in Exhibit 4.5. (To date, ARDI has not been able to obtain national for-profit or government salary surveys that analyze the difference between male and female compensation for the benchmark positions.)

Exhibit 4.5   Nonprofit Salaries—Gender Comparison

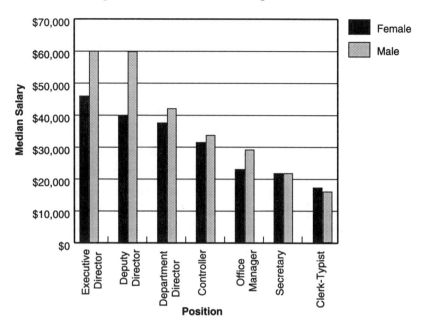

Source: Based on information from the Kansas City (8), Northern California (18), and Delaware (12) surveys.

Individual Position Comparisons

The information in this section is organized by the eight bench-mark positions. Each individual position section includes the following:

- A generic position description that can be applied to all sectors
- Alternate position titles from each of the sectors (shows the positions from each sector used for comparison)
- Expanded salary data (average, 25th percentile, median, and 75th percentile) by budget size for the nonprofit sector
- Gender comparisons of salaries for the nonprofit sector

- A bar chart showing median and average annual salaries across the sectors
- Key findings

Executive Director

Position Description

The **executive director** is responsible to the board of directors, or executive branch of government, for the growth and success of an organization or agency. Duties include advising and assisting in policy formulation, implementing policies and procedures, overseeing the organization's operations, and being a spokesperson to the public. (See Exhibits 4.6 and 4.7.)

Alternate Position Titles—Executive Director

Nonprofit:	Executive Director, Chief Executive Officer
For-profit:	Chief Executive Officer
Federal:	Level I position (examples):
	Secretary of State
	Secretary of the Interior
	Secretary of Agriculture
	Secretary of Health and Human Services
	Secretary of Education
State:	State Agency Head, State Department Director (examples):
	Division of Motor Vehicles Director
	Director of Personnel
Local (City/County):	City Manager
	County Manager

Salary Data

Exhibit 4.6 Nonprofit Salaries by Budget Size—Executive Director

Budget Size	$0–$99,999	$100,000–$249,000	$250,000–$499,000	$500,000–$999,999	$1M–$1,999,999	$2M–$4,999,999	Over $5,000,000
Average	$29,156	$33,098	$43,004	$54,644	$65,997	$81,161	$126,206
25th percentile	$27,633	$32,000	$39,615	$49,445	$56,062	$70,465	$ 92,057
Median	$29,156	$33,821	$43,700	$54,000	$59,093	$76,170	$107,448
75th percentile	$30,678	$35,000	$46,400	$56,258	$71,500	$86,177	$157,296

Overall Median: $57,320

Overall Average: $66,889

Nonprofit Median Salaries by Gender—Executive Director

The following median salaries are based on data from the Kansas City (8), Northern California (18), and Delaware (12) surveys.

Female: $44,863

Male: $60,008

	Median	Average
Nonprofit	$57,320	$66,889
For-profit (<$100M)	$187,265	$187,265
For-profit (>$100M)	$336,434	$336,434
Federal	$148,400	$148,400
State	$76,554	$79,657
Local (City/County)	$73,332	$71,823

Key Findings—Executive Director

- The order from lowest to highest median salary is nonprofit, local government, state government, federal government, and for-profit. This remains unchanged since the 1990 cross-sector comparison study.

Exhibit 4.7   Cross-Sector Comparison—Executive Director

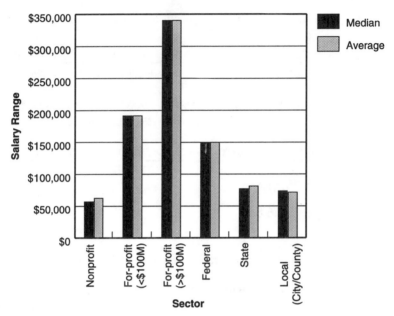

- Median annual salaries for nonprofit executive directors increased from $42,741 in 1989 to $57,320 in 1996, a 34 percent increase or approximately 4 percent compounded each year.

- The gap in actual dollars between overall executive director median salaries for the nonprofit and for-profit sectors is $191,755, the largest gap for any of the eight positions analyzed. The gap is not as great when the median salaries of larger nonprofits (budget sizes of $5,000,000 or more annually) are compared to the median salaries of for-profit organizations with sales volume less than $100,000,000 annually—$107,448 for the nonprofits and $187,265 in for-profit organizations, a gap of $79,817 per year.

- Based on median salary data from the three surveys that analyze salaries by gender, male executive directors in the nonprofit sector make 34 percent more than their female counterparts.

Deputy Director

Position Description

The **deputy director** is the executive responsible for coordinating, implementing, and directing policies and procedures assigned by the executive director. (See Exhibits 4.8 and 4.9.)

Alternate Position Titles—Deputy Director

Nonprofit:	Deputy/Associate Director, Deputy Chief Executive Officer
For-profit:	Chief Operating Officer
Federal:	Level II position (examples):
	Deputy Secretary of State
	Deputy Secretary of Agriculture
	Deputy Secretary of Labor
	Director of the Office of Personnel Management
State:	Deputy/Assistant Director of a state agency or department
Local (City/County):	Deputy/Assistant City Manager

Salary Data

Exhibit 4.8   Nonprofit Salaries by Budget Size—Deputy Director

Budget Size	$0–$99,999	$100,000–$249,000	$250,000–$499,000	$500,000–$999,999	$1M–$1,999,999	$2M–$4,999,999	Over $5,000,000
Average	$23,250	$25,920	$33,582	$40,770	$49,161	$58,738	$93,509
25th percentile	$23,250	$23,413	$31,377	$34,663	$38,762	$51,512	$73,500
Median	$23,250	$28,100	$33,754	$37,400	$49,024	$56,614	$82,000
75th percentile	$23,250	$29,517	$35,873	$42,775	$57,750	$63,642	$105,100

Overall Median: $46,025

Overall Average: $52,044

Nonprofit Median Salaries by Gender—Deputy Director

The following median salaries are based on data from the Kansas City (8) and Northern California (18) surveys.

Female: $39,458
Male: $60,064

Cross-Sector Median and Average Annual Salaries

	Median	*Average*
Nonprofit	$46,025	$52,044
For-profit (<$100M)	$157,827	$157,827
For-profit (>$100M)	$247,160	$247,160
Federal	$133,600	$133,600
State	$67,740	$67,740
Local (City/County):	$61,039	$61,253

Exhibit 4.9   Cross-Sector Comparison—Deputy Director

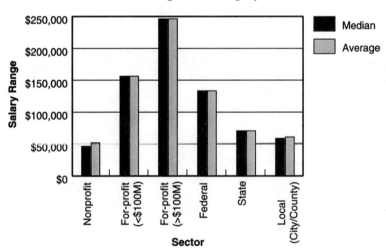

Key Findings—Deputy Director

- The order from lowest to highest median salary is non-profit, local government, state government, federal government, and for-profit. This remains virtually unchanged since the 1990 study, with state government now having higher salaries than local government as the only difference for this position.

- Median annual salaries for nonprofit deputy directors increased from $36,612 in 1989 to $46,025 in 1996, a 26 percent increase.

- The gap between overall median salaries for the nonprofit and for-profit sectors is $146,810, the second largest gap for any of the eight positions analyzed. Again, the gap is not as great as when the median salaries of larger nonprofits (budget sizes of $5,000,000 or more annually) are compared to the median salaries of for-profit organizations with sales volume less than $100,000,000 annually—$82,000 for the nonprofits and $157,827 in for-profit organizations, a gap of $75,827 per year.

- Based on the two surveys that break out gender data, male deputy directors in the nonprofit sector make 52 percent more than their female counterparts.

Department Director

Position Description

The **department director** is the executive responsible for coordinating, implementing, and directing the efforts in one particular area or division of an organization or an agency. This person works with the executive director and supervises the activities of other professionals to achieve the organization's goals. (See Exhibits 4.10 and 4.11.)

Alternate Position Titles—Department Director

Nonprofit:	Department Director, Top Program Officer (examples):
	Director of Human Resources
	Director of Public Relations
	Director of Program(s)
	Director of Operations
For-profit:	Top Department Executive (examples):
	Director of Marketing
	Director of Manufacturing
	Director of Personnel
Federal:	Level III position (examples):
	Under Secretary of Education
	Administrator of General Services Director
	Chairman of the National Endowment for the Humanities
State:	Division Director
	Chief of Classification
	Security Director
Local (City/County):	Agency Director (examples):
	Finance Director
	Personnel Director
	Planning Director

Salary Data

Exhibit 4.10 Nonprofit Salaries by Budget Size—Department Director

Budget Size	$0–$99,999	$100,000–$249,000	$250,000–$499,000	$500,000–$999,999	$1M–$1,999,999	$2M–$4,999,999	Over $5,000,000
Average	$28,833	$22,337	$25,647	$32,102	$35,469	$44,188	$54,911
25th percentile	$28,833	$20,745	$24,184	$30,196	$31,923	$36,024	$41,226
Median	$28,833	$23,489	$25,850	$31,791	$36,000	$40,384	$49,168
75th percentile	$28,833	$24,505	$27,313	$34,793	$40,519	$54,200	$72,025

Overall Median: $33,130
Overall Average: $37,591

Nonprofit Median Salaries by Gender—Department Director

The following median salaries are based on data from the Kansas City (8) and Northern California (18) surveys.

Female: $36,947
Male: $42,955

Cross-Sector Median and Average Annual Salaries

	Median	*Average*
Nonprofit	$33,130	$37,591
For-profit (<$100M)	$85,950	$83,845
For-profit (>$100M)	$91,663	$91,663
Federal	$123,100	$123,100
State	$40,055	$40,055
Local (City/County)	$53,208	$53,721

Key Findings—Department Director

- The order from lowest to highest median salary is nonprofit, state government, local government, for-profit, and federal government. This is the only position in which the for-profit sector does not have the highest annual median salary.

- Median annual salaries for nonprofit department directors increased from $27,403 in 1989 to $33,130 in 1996, a 20 percent increase.

- The gap between overall median salaries for the nonprofit and the federal government (the highest sector for this position) is $89,970.

Exhibit 4.11 Cross-Sector Comparison—Department Director

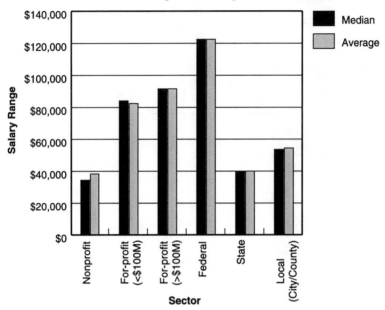

- Based on the two surveys that break out gender data, male department directors in the nonprofit sector make 16 percent more than their female counterparts.

Controller

Position Description

The **controller** is the executive responsible for directing the organization's accounting practices, maintaining financial records, and preparing financial management reports and procedures. Duties include supervision of all accounting and budget functions, collection and analysis of statistical and accounting information, and other activities that impact the fiscal stability and effective operation of the organization. In smaller nonprofit organizations, this position is also often referred to as the chief financial officer (CFO). This terminology does not hold true in the for-profit sector where CFOs are supervisory to controllers. (See Exhibits 4.12 and 4.13.)

Alternate Position Titles—Controller

Nonprofit:	Controller, Chief/Top Financial Officer
For-profit:	Controller
Federal:	Financial Manager GS-505-13
State:	Comptroller II, Accountant IV
Local (City/County):	Controller, Accountant Senior Level

Salary Data

Exhibit 4.12   Nonprofit Salaries by Budget Size—Controller

Budget Size	$0–$99,999	$100,000–$249,000	$250,000–$499,000	$500,000–$999,999	$1M–$1,999,999	$2M–$4,999,999	Over $5,000,000
Average	——	——	$27,362	$34,304	$37,882	$43,894	$66,378
25th percentile	——	——	$22,266	$29,627	$32,200	$38,736	$54,439
Median	——	——	$26,667	$33,764	$34,575	$42,053	$58,240
75th percentile	——	——	$31,763	$38,405	$43,187	$48,788	$76,037

Overall Median: $40,032
Overall Average: $42,589

Nonprofit Median Salaries by Gender—Controller

The following median salaries are based on data from the Kansas City (8) and Northern California (18) surveys.

Female: $32,252
Male: $35,126

Cross-Sector Median and Average Annual Salaries

	Median	Average
Nonprofit	$40,032	$42,589
For-profit (<$100M)	$61,818	$60,459

	Median	*Average*
For-profit (>$100M)	$93,800	$93,800
Federal	$58,838	$58,838
State	$51,674	$51,674
Local (City/County)	$38,507	$38,496

Key Findings—Controller

- The order from lowest to highest median salary is local government, nonprofit, state government, federal government, and for-profit. This is one of three positions in which the

Exhibit 4.13   Cross-Sector Comparison—Controller

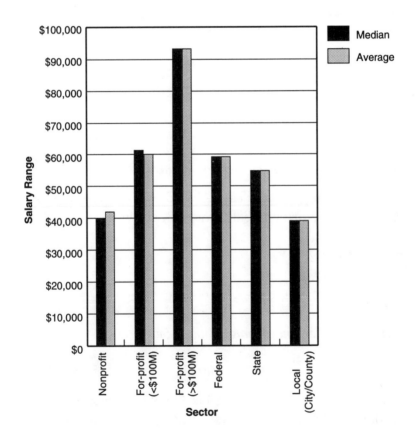

nonprofit sector does not have the lowest annual median salary (the other two are bookkeeper and clerk-typist).

- Median annual salaries for nonprofit controllers increased from $31,094 in 1989 to $40,032 in 1996, a 28 percent increase.

- The gap between overall median salaries for the nonprofit and for-profit sectors is $31,368. The gap is very small when the median salaries of larger nonprofits (budget sizes of $5,000,000 or more annually) are compared to the median salaries of for-profit organizations with sales volume less than $100,000,000 annually—$58,240 for the nonprofits and $61,818 in for-profit organizations, a gap of $3,578 per year.

- Based on the two surveys that break out gender data, male controllers in the nonprofit sector make 8 percent more than their female counterparts. This difference is considerably less than the executive-level variation, and this trend continues throughout the remainder of the positions.

Bookkeeper

Position Description

The **bookkeeper** is the person who maintains accounting records and files. Responsibilities include preparing financial records and other relevant financial statements and analyzing data. (See Exhibits 4.14 and 4.15.)

Alternate Position Titles—Bookkeeper

Nonprofit:	Bookkeeper, Account Clerk
For-profit:	Accounting Clerk
Federal:	Accounting Technician GS-525-5
State:	Accounting Clerk II, III
Local (City/County):	Bookkeeper, Account Clerk

Salary Data

Exhibit 4.14   Nonprofit Salaries by Budget Size—Bookkeeper

Budget Size	$0– $99,999	$100,000– $249,000	$250,000– $499,000	$500,000– $999,999	$1M– $1,999,999	$2M– $4,999,999	Over $5,000,000
Average	——	$20,068	$21,530	$21,879	$21,427	$21,576	$22,236
25th percentile	——	$18,601	$19,815	$19,238	$20,800	$20,808	$21,403
Median	——	$20,068	$21,530	$22,000	$21,500	$21,309	$22,755
75th percentile	——	$21,534	$23,245	$23,935	$22,358	$22,131	$23,588

Overall Median: $22,000
Overall Average: $21,589

Nonprofit Median Salaries by Gender—Bookkeeper

The following median salaries are based on data from the Kansas City (8) and Northern California (18) surveys.

Female: $22,905
Male: $24,690

Cross-Sector Median and Average Annual Salaries

	Median	Average
Nonprofit	$22,000	$21,589
For-profit (<$100M)	$23,610	$23,610
Federal	$22,518	$22,518
State	$21,133	$21,796
Local (City/County)	$23,160	$23,544

Key Findings—Bookkeeper

- The order from lowest to highest median salary is state government, nonprofit, federal government, local government, and for-profit.

Exhibit 4.15   Cross-Sector Comparison—Bookkeeper

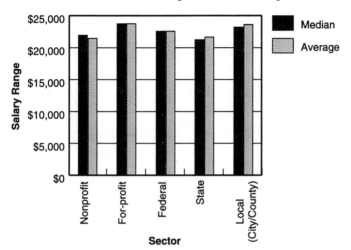

- Median annual salaries for nonprofit bookkeepers increased from $16,918 in 1989 to $22,000 in 1996, a 30 percent increase.

- The gap between overall median salaries for the nonprofit and for-profit sectors is very small at $1,610. Unlike the previous four managerial or professional positions, the gap changes very little when larger nonprofits and smaller for-profits are compared.

- Based on the two surveys that break out gender data, male bookkeepers in the nonprofit sector make 7 percent more than their female counterparts.

Office Manager

Position Description

The **office manager** is responsible for general office services, including the supervision of office personnel, scheduling workload, maintenance of equipment, and ordering supplies. This person may also be responsible for clerical, accounting, and sales functions. (See Exhibits 4.16 and 4.17.)

Alternate Position Titles—Office Manager

Nonprofit: Office Manager

For-profit: Office Manager, Manager-Office
                              Services

Federal: Support Services Administrator GS-
                              342-8

State: Office Supervisor, Business Manager I,
                              Administrative Assistant II

Local (City/County):   Supervisor-Office, Executive/Admin-
                              istrative Secretary, Assistant City
                              Clerk

Salary Data

Exhibit 4.16   Nonprofit Salaries by Budget Size—Office Manager

Budget Size	$0–$99,999	$100,000–$249,000	$250,000–$499,000	$500,000–$999,999	$1M–$1,999,999	$2M–$4,999,999	Over $5,000,000
Average	——	$16,064	$19,133	$23,957	$28,293	$29,666	$34,694
25th percentile	——	$15,035	$17,350	$20,375	$23,938	$28,721	$26,351
Median	——	$16,064	$18,700	$24,000	$26,875	$29,517	$29,207
75th percentile	——	$17,092	$20,700	$25,251	$31,988	$31,947	$36,891

Overall Median: $25,740
Overall Average: $27,330

Nonprofit Median Salaries by Gender—Office Manager

The following median salaries are based on data from the Kansas City (8) and Northern California (18) surveys.

Female: $23,700
Male: $28,652

Cross-Sector Median and Average Annual Salaries

	Median	Average
Nonprofit	$25,740	$27,330
For-profit (<$100M)	$39,550	$39,550
Federal	$30,892	$30,892
State	$28,164	$32,709
Local (City/County)	$29,553	$30,647

Key Findings—Office Manager

- The order from lowest to highest median salary is nonprofit, state government, local government, federal government, and for-profit.

- Median annual salaries for nonprofit office managers in-

Exhibit 4.17   Cross-Sector Comparison—Office Manager

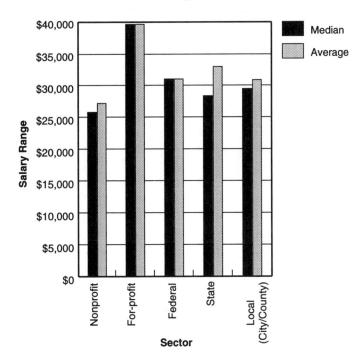

creased from $19,857 in 1989 to $25,740 in 1996, a 29 percent increase.

- The gap between overall median salaries for the nonprofit and for-profit sectors is $13,810. As is the case with all of the technical and clerical positions, the gap changes very little when larger nonprofits and smaller for-profits are compared.

- Based on the two surveys that break out gender data, male office managers in the nonprofit sector make 20 percent more than their female counterparts.

Secretary

Position Description

The **secretary** performs a variety of clerical and typing duties and provides support to one or several professionals or managers. Typical duties include typing letters and reports, answering phone calls, maintaining files, arranging meetings, and keeping records. (See Exhibitis 4.18 and 4.19.)

Alternate Position Titles—Secretary

Nonprofit:	Secretary
For-profit:	Secretary, Secretary B/I
Federal:	Secretary GS-318-5
State:	Secretary, Secretary II
Local (City/County):	Secretary

Salary Data

Exhibit 4.18   Nonprofit Salaries by Budget Size—Secretary

Budget Size	$0–$99,999	$100,000–$249,000	$250,000–$499,000	$500,000–$999,999	$1M–$1,999,999	$2M–$4,999,999	Over $5,000,000
Average	$15,750	$15,232	$17,544	$18,122	$19,106	$20,998	$22,312
25th percentile	$15,750	$14,166	$16,333	$16,389	$16,437	$18,012	$20,382
Median	$15,750	$15,232	$17,000	$17,702	$18,800	$19,375	$22,480
75th percentile	$15,750	$16,298	$18,714	$19,950	$21,160	$22,988	$24,378

Overall Median: $18,047
Overall Average: $19,189

Nonprofit Median Salaries by Gender—Secretary

The following median salaries are based on data from the Kansas City (8) and Northern California (18) surveys.

Female: $22,160
Male: $22,345

Cross-Sector Median and Average Annual Salaries

	Median	*Average*
Nonprofit	$18,047	$19,189
For-profit (<$100M)	$22,953	$23,367
Federal	$22,518	$22,518
State	$21,067	$22,342
Local (City/County)	$21,576	$21,433

Exhibit 4.19   Cross-Sector Comparison—Secretary

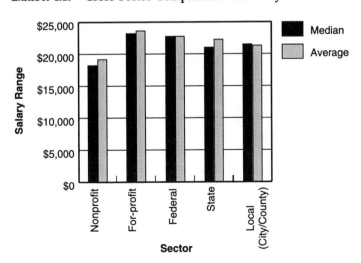

Key Findings—Secretary

- The order from lowest to highest median salary is non-profit, state government, local government, federal government, and for-profit.

- Median annual salaries for nonprofit secretaries increased from $15,887 in 1989 to $18,047 in 1996, a 13.5 percent increase.

- The gap between overall median salaries for the nonprofit and for-profit sectors is $4,906.

- Based on the two surveys that break out gender data, male secretaries in the nonprofit sector make 1 percent more than their female counterparts.

Clerk-Typist

Position Description

The **clerk-typist** performs clerical duties, answers incoming calls, places outgoing calls, and receives visitors and directs them to the appropriate person or office. This person typically performs a variety of clerical support and public relations functions under the direct supervision of the office manager. (See Exhibits 4.20 and 4.21.)

Alternate Position Titles—Clerk-Typist

Nonprofit:	Clerk-Typist, Receptionist
For-profit:	Clerk-Typist, Receptionist
Federal:	Clerk-Typist GS-322-3
State:	Clerk-Typist, Clerk-General, Clerk II
Local (City/County):	Clerk-Typist, Administrative Clerk

Salary Data

Exhibit 4.20   Nonprofit Salaries by Budget Size—Clerk-Typist

Budget Size	$0–$99,999	$100,000–$249,000	$250,000–$499,000	$500,000–$999,999	$1M–$1,999,999	$2M–$4,999,999	Over $5,000,000
Average	—	—	—	$15,330	$16,306	$15,112	$17,378
25th percentile	—	—	—	$14,415	$15,650	$14,672	$16,059
Median	—	—	—	$15,330	$16,000	$15,560	$16,227
75th percentile	—	—	—	$16,245	$16,809	$16,000	$18,121

Overall Median: $15,946
Overall Average: $16,013

Nonprofit Median Salaries by Gender—Clerk-Typist

The following median salaries are based on data from the Kansas City (8) and Northern California (18) surveys.

Female: $16,414
Male: $14,863

Cross-Sector Median and Average Annual Salaries

	Median	Average
Nonprofit	$15,946	$16,013
For-profit (<$100M)	$18,856	$19,344
Federal	$17,928	$17,928
State	$15,576	$16,642
Local (City/County)	$18,528	$18,738

Key Findings—Clerk Typist

- The order from lowest to highest median salary is state government, nonprofit, federal government, local government, and for-profit.

Exhibit 4.21   Cross-Sector Comparison—Clerk-Typist

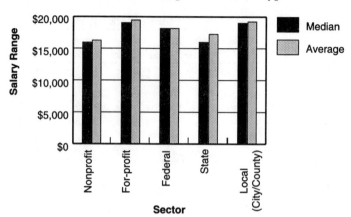

- Median annual salaries for nonprofit clerk-typists increased from $13,078 in 1989 to $15,946 in 1996, a 22 percent increase.

- The gap between overall median salaries for the nonprofit and for-profit sectors is $2,910.

- Based on the two surveys that break out gender data, male clerk-typists in the nonprofit sector make 10 percent *less* than their female counterparts. This was the only position in which men earned less than women in the nonprofit sector.

RESULTS—CROSS-SECTOR BENEFITS ANALYSIS AND COMPARISON

This section includes an analysis of various benefit options found in the nonprofit, for-profit, and government sectors. The benefits are grouped and reported on by type, including

- Health
- Life and disability
- Leave

- Retirement
- Other

When ARDI conducted its initial cross-sector compensation study in 1990, there was not a great deal of available survey data that focused on benefits in the workplace. This was especially true of the nonprofit sector. Fortunately, this is no longer the case, and most compensation surveys include more detailed information on benefits.

Many nonprofit organizations have begun to use innovative compensation practices in order to compete with the other sectors in recruiting and retaining employees. For example, benefit practices that ARDI considers to be innovative include flexible spending accounts, job-sharing, and premium conversion plans, among others. Information on these innovative practices is not widely reported on; however, ARDI conducted a study in 1993 that identified innovative cash and benefit practices that nonprofit organizations are using. Information from this 1993 study can be found in Chapter Five.

The exhibits and discussion in this section show the percentage of organizations, agencies, states, municipalities, and so on, that offer traditional benefit options. Even though benefit information is now more prevalent, there are still gaps and limited data on some of the benefit types. It is unclear whether these gaps mean that the benefits are not offered by a given sector or that they are still not reported. For the purpose of analysis, this study assumes that the benefits exist only as reported.

Following are some overall perceptions of the benefits comparison between sectors. More detailed findings are included in the individual benefit-type analyses.

- Nonprofit health benefit packages compare favorably with other sectors. However, as in the previous study, nonprofit organizations still lag in terms of retiree medical coverage.
- More government and for-profit organizations offer life insurance coverage to their employees than do nonprofit

organizations. However, in the case of accidental death and *long-term* disability insurance coverage, the nonprofit sector compares favorably to the for-profit, state, and local government sectors.

- Leave benefits in the nonprofit sector are typically more generous than in the for-profit sector and on a par with the government sectors. On average, nonprofit organizations offer twelve vacation days per year after one year of service. Many nonprofit organizations (31 percent) offer fifteen vacation days per year after one year of service, which is considerably more than the other sectors.

- As was the case in the 1990 cross-sector comparison, the nonprofit sector in general does not offer as many retiree benefits to employees as the other sectors do in 1996. This situation holds true for health, life, and disability insurance and retirement benefits.

- Overall, nonprofit organizations are now offering more benefit options to their employees than was the case in 1989.

Health Benefits

Exhibit 4.22 shows the percentage of organizations, agencies, states, and municipalities that offer health benefits to their employees. Row 1, "Offers medical," denotes that the organization offers some form of basic medical insurance. Many organizations pay 100 percent of the medical insurance for their employees—Row 2 shows the percentage of organizations that offer full coverage. Rows 3a–c, "Types of coverage offered," show the variety of medical insurance options available to employees. In some cases, the organizations offer more than one type of coverage, thus the percentages in Rows 3a–c may not total 100 percent. Rows 4 through 8 provide information on other health insurance options offered by organizations. The organizations may pay all or a portion of the premiums, with the employees contributing the rest.

Exhibit 4.22   Health Benefits Comparative Analysis

	Nonprofit	For-profit	Federal	State	Local (City/County)
1. Offers medical	91%	82%	100%	87%	94%
2. Pays 100% of coverage	53%	40%	(pays 60%)	——	68%
3. Types of coverage offered:					
a. Major medical	40%	——	——	38%	38%
b. HMO	46%	21%	optional	——	——
c. PPO	34%	25%	optional	30%	46%
4. Offers vision	20%	18%	—	30%	30%
5. Offers dental	62%	45%	——	35%	40%
6. Flexible benefits plan	27%	24%	——	62%	64%
7. Retiree medical coverage	7%	41%	100% (pays 60%)	——	——
8. Dependent coverage	44%	92%	100% (pays 60%)	——	64%

Definitions—Health Benefits

Major Medical—Plans that pay benefits for a wide range of medical expenses, including inpatient/outpatient services, prescriptions, wellness benefits, and typically some form of life insurance coverage. These plans also offer protection for large, unpredictable medical expenses. Patients have an unlimited choice of physicians and hospitals. Often referred to as traditional indemnity plans or comprehensive coverage.

HMO (Health Maintenance Organization)—Plans that include a variety of coverage and payment options. HMOs consist of a network of hospitals and physicians, and patients must see a designated primary care physician and/or attend a designated hospital within this network.

PPO (Preferred Provider Organization)—Similar to an HMO in that there is a network of hospitals and physicians. However, patients are not required to see a designated physician or attend a network hospital, although cost savings are realized when patients stay within the network.

Flexible Benefits Plans—Plans that allow an employer to offer a variety of benefit options for employees, such as health, dental, vision, term-life, and disability insurance; prepaid legal services; child care; and medical or dental reimbursement. These options are selected and paid for by the employee with pre-tax dollars through salary reduction.

Key Findings—Health Benefits

- Data on nonprofit health benefits are now more readily available than it was in 1990.
- Some form of medical insurance coverage is offered by 91 percent of nonprofit organizations. Fifty-three percent of the nonprofit organizations offering insurance pay the entire premium for their employees.
- The 1990 cross-sector comparison study found health benefits data that distinguished between professional level and support staff. ARDI did not find similar distinctions in 1996. For comparison's sake, the 1990 study showed that 87 percent of professional staff and 77 percent of support staff were offered basic medical insurance (based on data from 1989) versus the 91 percent total figure in 1996.

Life and Disability Benefits

Exhibit 4.23 shows the percentage of organizations, agencies, states, and municipalities that offer life and disability benefits.

Exhibit 4.23   Life and Disability Benefits—Comparative Analysis

	Nonprofit	For-profit	Federal	State	Local (City/County)
Life insurance	56%	76%	100% (pays 33%)	87%	91%
Dependent life insurance	19%	9%	optional (unpaid)	46%	46%
Supplemental life insur.	18%	38%	optional (unpaid)	55%	55%
Accidental death/dismem.	60%	59%	100% (pays 33%)	56%	56%
Travel insurance	30%	29%	——	13%	——
Retiree life insurance	10%	21%	100% (unpaid)	46%	45%
Disability (short-term)	31%	74%	——	95%	95%
Disability (long-term)	48%	31%	100%	30%	39%
Disability (both)	26%	——	——	——	——

The organizations providing insurance coverage may pay all or a portion of the premium.

Definitions—Life and Disability Benefits

Life Insurance—This category includes a variety of plan options, but typically refers to a basic group life plan. However, the percentages shown in Exhibit 4.23 simply refer to the fact that some form of life insurance is offered and do not distinguish between plan types.

Dependent Life Insurance—The organization offers life insurance options to family members (may be paid or unpaid).

Supplemental Life Insurance—The organization offers the option of obtaining coverage in addition to the regular group plan. Almost always paid for by the employee and usually offered to executive level employees only.

Disability (both)—The organization offers a combination plan including long-term *and* short-term disability insurance.

Key Findings—Life and Disability Benefits

- As is the case with health benefits, data on nonprofit life and disability benefits is more readily available than in the past.
- Some form of life insurance coverage is offered by 56 percent of nonprofit organizations. This percentage is considerably lower than in the other sectors.
- The percentage of nonprofit organizations offering life and disability insurance has declined approximately 7 percent since the 1990 study.
- Retiree life insurance coverage is offered by a smaller percentage of nonprofit organizations than in the other sectors. This appears to be a trend in terms of retiree benefits

in general—nonprofits do not offer as many benefit options to their retirees as other sectors do.

Leave Benefits

Vacation

Exhibit 4.24, Row 1, "Vacation after 1 yr.," shows the number of vacation days provided to employees after one year of service. Rows 1a–d show the percentage of organizations offering one,

Exhibit 4.24   Vacation Days—Comparative Analysis

	Nonprofit	For-profit	Federal	State	Local (City/County)
Exempt Employees					
1. Vacation after 1 yr.:	12 days	10 days	13 days	13 days	11 days
a. 1 week	13%	18%	——	4%	4%
b. 2 weeks	47%	57%	——	29%	29%
c. 3 weeks	31%	8%	——	12%	12%
d. 4 weeks	7%	4%	——	4%	4%
e. 5 weeks	——	2%	——	0%	0%
2. Vacation after 2 yrs.:	18 days	——	13 days	——	——
3. Vacation after 3 yrs.:	16 days	12 days	20 days	14 days	12 days
4. Vacation after 4 yrs.:	19 days	——	20 days	——	——
5. Vacation after 5 yrs.:	20 days	14 days	20 days	16 days	14 days
a. 1 week	1%	5%	——	0%	0%
b. 2 weeks	9%	30%	——	13%	13%
c. 3 weeks	46%	41%	——	32%	32%
d. 4 weeks	18%	7%	100%	8%	8%
e. 5 weeks	2%	4%	——	0%	0%
Nonexempt Employees					
6. Vacation after 1 yr.:	9 days	9 days	13 days	12 days	12 days
a. 1 week	7%	36%	——	9%	9%
b. 2 weeks	60%	53%	——	41%	41%
c. 3 weeks	3%	2%	——	4%	4%
d. 4 weeks	1%	1%	——	4%	4%
e. 5 weeks	——	1%	——	1%	1%
7. Vacation after 5 yrs.:	14 days	13 days	20 days	15 days	15 days
a. 1 week	1%	5%	——	1%	1%
b. 2 weeks	11%	43%	——	23%	23%
c. 3 weeks	36%	39%	——	31%	31%
d. 4 weeks	16%	3%	100%	5%	5%
e. 5 weeks	3%	1%	——	1%	1%

two, three, four, or five weeks of vacation after one year of service. For example, in the nonprofit column, Row 1a shows that 13 percent of all organizations provide one week of vacation after one year of service. The data is separated into "Exempt" and "Nonexempt" employee categories.

Paid Holidays

In addition to vacation days, there are paid holidays in every work situation. Exhibit 4.25 shows the average number of holidays for each category.

Sick Leave

Employees are allowed paid days for sick leave. Exhibit 4.26 shows numbers of sick leave days.

Miscellaneous Leave

Exhibit 4.27 shows the percentage of organizations that offer a given type of leave and the corresponding number of leave days allowed in a year for that type. In most cases, this represents paid time off. For example, in the nonprofit sector 85 percent of the organizations provide bereavement leave, and the average number of days allowed per year for bereavement leave is five.

Exhibit 4.25   Paid Holidays

	Nonprofit	For-profit	Federal	State	Local
Holidays observed per yr.	11 days	10 days	10 days	12 days	11 days

Exhibit 4.26   Paid Sick Days

	Nonprofit	For-profit	Federal	State	Local
Sick days available per yr.	11 days	11 days	13 days	13 days	13 days

Exhibit 4.27   Miscellaneous Leave—Comparative Analysis

	Nonprofit	For-profit	Federal	State	Local
Paid Leave					
Bereavement (% offering)	85%	67%	0%	62%	72%
			(can use sick leave.)		
Bereavement days per yr.	5	3	——	4	3
Jury (% offering)	85%	74%	100%	94%	94%
Jury days per yr.	as needed	as needed	as needed	as needed	as needed
Military (% offering)	43%	35%	100%	75%	75%
Military days per yr.	13	13	15	14	14
Unpaid Leave					
Maternity (% offering)	52%	3%	——	——	——
Maternity days per yr.	44	——	——	——	——
Paternity (% offering)	40%	1%	——	——	——
Paternity days per yr.	36	——	——	——	——
Personal (% offering)	63%	17%	——	38%	66%
Personal days per yr.	1	3	——	3	3
Family (% offering)	——	——	100%	93%	93%
Family days per yr.	——	——	60	——	——

Key Findings—Leave Benefits

- Nonprofit organizations allow an average of 12 vacation days off per year after one year of service. This is higher than the more traditional 10 days off per year found in the for-profit sector. After five years of service, nonprofits offer 20 days off, versus 14 in the for-profit sector.

- After the first year of service, most nonprofit organizations (47 percent) offer 2 weeks of vacation. However, another 31 percent of nonprofit organizations offer 3 weeks of vacation after one year of service, which is considerably more generous than the corresponding data found in the other sectors.

- Overall, vacation leave for exempt employees in the nonprofit sector is on a par with the federal government and more generous than the for-profit, state, and local sectors; however, this is not the case for nonexempt employees. The nonprofit and for-profit sectors lag behind the government sectors in terms of vacation time for nonexempt personnel.

- Holidays and sick leave are relatively even among the sectors, varying only by one to two days per year.

- Federal, state, and local government agencies and organizations offer a higher percentage of miscellaneous leave (jury, personal, family, etc.) than do the nonprofit and for-profit sectors (i.e., more types of leave and more days for each type).

- Paid maternity and paternity leave and also unpaid maternity leave show up frequently in nonprofit benefit data. This is not the case in the business and government sectors. In these sectors, the predominant means of dealing with family issues such as a newborn is through a general *unpaid* family leave plan. Family leave can be applied to a variety of situations such as caring for a sick family member, taking care of a newborn, or health problems that prevent the employee from adequately performing their duties. With the exception of government, data on the number of organizations offering family leave and the number of days offered was unavailable in the surveys that ARDI was able to obtain.

Retirement Benefits

Exhibit 4.28 details the percentage of organizations, agencies, states, etc. within each sector that provide some form of retirement plan for their employees. The chart further details the types of plans offered. Information on the amount contributed to the plans by the employers was difficult to quantify; therefore the chart simply shows percentage of organizations offering the plans.

Definitions—Retirement Benefits

Defined-Benefit Pension—Pension plan that requires that an employer provide a retirement benefit calculated by a formula that

Exhibit 4.28   Retirement Benefits—Comparative Analysis

	Nonprofit	For-profit	Federal	State	Local (City/County)
Offer retirement plans	59%	60%	100%	96%	96%
Types of plans offered					
Defined-benefit pension	28%	36%	100%	91%	85%
Defined-contribution pension	22%	42%	optional	9%	15%
Profit sharing	——	13%	——	——	——
401K	——	28%	——	——	——
Thrift savings plan	——	——	optional	——	——
403B (tax-sheltered annuities)	48%	——	——	——	——
Other plans	21%	——	——	——	——
Supplemental exec. plan	16%	——	——	——	——

is specified in the plan. Benefits are typically based on salary, years of service, or both. In most cases, employees do not contribute their own funds to defined-benefit plans.

Defined-Contribution Pension—Pension plan that usually specifies the level of the employer contribution to the plan, but not the formula for determining eventual benefits as in a defined-benefit plan. Employees may contribute to most of these plans, and employers may match all or a portion of the employee's contribution. Types of defined-contribution plans are:

- Savings and thrift plans
- Cash or deferred arrangements, such as 401(k)s
- Employee stock-ownership plans
- Deferred profit sharing

401(k)—Often referred to as a salary reduction plan, allows participants to choose between receiving currently taxable income or deferring taxation by placing the money in a retirement account; 401(k) plans may include employer contributions. This type of plan has not been available to nonprofit organizations in the past. However, as of 1997, tax-exempt employers other than state and local governments can offer 401(k)s to their employees.

403(b)—Often referred to as a Tax Sheltered Annuity, allows employees of certain tax-exempt institutions to reduce their taxable income by setting aside pretax dollars in a retirement account (may *not* include employer contributions).

Supplemental Executive Plans—Special plans (may be any type) that are typically offered to managerial-level employees. These plans allow the employee additional retirement or investment options, but usually not additional funds for these purposes.

Key Findings—Retirement Benefits

- Approximately 60 percent of nonprofit and for-profit organizations offer retirement benefits to their employees. This represents a 15 percent increase in organizations offering these benefits in the nonprofit sector since the 1990 study. However, the current percentage is much lower than the 96 percent currently found in state and local governments and the 100 percent found in the federal government.
- Defined-benefit plans are the predominant type of retirement plan in the government sector, while the nonprofit and for-profit sectors offer a relatively equal number of defined-benefit and defined-contribution plans.
- Within the nonprofit sector, the most common retirement plan is a Tax-Sheltered Annuity (TSA)—of those nonprofit organizations offering retirement plans, 48 percent chose a TSA.

Other Benefits

Exhibit 4.29 covers a variety of benefit options available to employees. It shows the percentage of organizations offering a given benefit as reported in surveys.

Key Findings—Other Benefits

- As has been the case when analyzing the other benefit types, information on nonprofit benefits in this category is

Exhibit 4.29   Additional Benefits—Comparative Analysis

	Nonprofit	For-profit	Federal	State	Local (City/County)
Child care	9%	7%	——	48%	7%
Dependent care	3%	——	——	4%	——
Car: Business use	13%	——	——	——	——
Car: Personal use	——	——	——	——	——
Mileage reimbursement	95%	85%	100%	——	——
Moving expenses	25%	49%	——	——	——
Flextime	44%	—	100%	88%	——
Credit union	38%	——	——	——	——
Educational assistance	34%	72%	——	64%	64%
Bonuses	42%	——	——	34%	——
Stock purchase	——	——	——	——	——
Key person insurance	——	——	——	——	——
Special parking	62%	——	——	——	——
Financial/tax counseling	5%	25%	——	6%	6%
Personal liability insurance	——	——	——	——	——
Country/health club	12%	16%	——	14%	14%
Meals	18%	——	——	——	——
Professional dues	43%	——	——	——	——
Severance pay	36%	26%	100%	29%	29%

now more readily available than it was in 1990. Information was available for only four of the nineteen benefit types in 1990, compared to fifteen of nineteen in 1996.

- In the four nonprofit categories that can be compared over time, three have shown improvement:

	1989	1996
Child care	6%	9%
Flextime	33%	44%
Credit union	26%	38%

- The nonprofit sector compares favorably to the for-profit and government sectors in almost all the "other benefit" categories. The only notable difference occurs within educational assistance—34 percent of nonprofits offer educational assistance, compared to an average of 67 percent in the other sectors.

SUMMARY

The information in this chapter has provided important summary information on how the nonprofit sector compares with the for-profit sector and government in wages and benefits. These approaches to compensation are based more on traditional forms of compensation. However, other methods for compensating and motivating employees have been used in for-profit businesses in particular for some time. More recently, nonprofit organizations and even government have begun to consider and implement innovative approaches to compensation. These approaches have a variety of potential benefits, such as cost savings to the employer, closer relationships of rewards to performance, and greater flexibility to match employee interests. Implementation of innovative practices in compensation by nonprofits has been slow to date. This may be because nonprofits did not have the expertise to establish and administer them or even because the innovations might be viewed as inappropriate to the culture and ethics of nonprofits. Another factor is the ongoing concern about and confusion between expenses for "direct programs" versus compensation of employees. The resulting tension from this confusion is unnecessary as it is through employees that programs are provided, money is raised, and missions accomplished.

However, competition for qualified personnel and pressures for cost savings are strong driving forces for change. All nonprofits should learn more about these practices and consider them as compensation policies and practices are established or upgraded. Chapter Five provides information on innovative compensation trends and case-study experiences of nonprofits that have implemented different types of innovative compensation programs. This information together with the cross-sector-study information provided will give the readers a strong factual basis for their work on this area of their own organization.

REFERENCES

1. Abbott, Langer & Associates, *Compensation in Nonprofit Organizations, 9th Edition* (Crete, IL: Abbott, Langer & Associates, 1996).

2. Abbott, Langer & Associates, *Compensation of Chief Executive Officers in Nonprofit Organizations, 9th Edition* (Crete, IL: Abbott, Langer & Associates, 1996).

3. Association of Washington Cities, *Washington City and County Employee Salary and Benefits Survey for 1996* (Olympia, WA: Association of Washington Cities, 1996).

4. Bureau of Labor Statistics, "BLS Reports on Employee Benefits in State and Local Governments, 1994," *Bureau of Labor Statistics* (Online). Available: http://www.stats.bls.gov/ebs2.toc.htm.

5. Business & Legal Reports, Inc., *1996 Survey of Exempt Compensation* (Madison, CT: Business & Legal Reports, Inc., 1996).

6. Business & Legal Reports, Inc., *1996 Survey of Employee Benefits* (Madison, CT: Business & Legal Reports, Inc., 1996).

7. California Guide, *Collective Bargaining* (Sacramento, CA: California Guide, 1995).

8. Center for Management Assistance, *1995 Nonprofit Salary and Benefits Survey of the Greater Kansas City Area* (Kansas City, MO: Center for Management Assistance, 1995).

9. Colorado Municipal League, *Benchmark Employee Compensation Report* (Denver, CO: Colorado Municipal League, 1996).

10. Colorado Municipal League, *Management Compensation Report* (Denver, CO: Colorado Municipal League, 1996).

11. Council of State Government, *The Book of the States, 1996–97* (Vol. 31) (Lexington, KY: Council of State Government, 1996).

12. Delaware Association of Nonprofit Agencies, *Delaware Nonprofit Wage & Benefit Survey, 1996 Edition* (Wilmington, DE: Delaware Association of Nonprofit Agencies, 1996).

13. Ernst & Young LLP, *1995 Survey of New York Metropolitan Area Not-for-Profit Organizations, Compensation and Benefits* (New York: Ernst & Young LLP, 1996).

14. Ex Comp Service (ECS), *1995/1996, Top Management Report* (Rochelle Park, NJ: ECS, a Wyatt Data Services Company, 1996).

15. Federal Employees News Digest, "1996 General Schedule Pay Tables by Locality," *Federal Employees News Digest*, 1996.

16. Florida League of Cities, *Cooperative Salary Survey, Group II: Cities with 10,000 to 49,000 Population* (Tallahassee, FL: Florida League of Cities, 1996).

17. Don Mace and Eric Yoder, *Federal Employees Almanac, 1996, 43rd Edition* (Reston, VA: Federal Employees News Digest, Inc., 1996).

18. Management Center, *1996 Wage & Benefit Survey of Northern California Nonprofit Organizations* (San Francisco: The Management Center, 1996).

19. National Association of State Personnel, *State Personnel Office: Rules and Functions* (Lexington, KY: National Association of State Personnel, 1996).

20. National Collaboration for Youth, *Salaries and Benefits in Youth Development Agencies 1996* (Washington, DC: National Assembly of National Voluntary Health and Social Welfare Organizations, 1996).

21. Nebraska State Government, *Salary Survey* (Lincoln, NE: Personnel Division, 1996).

22. State of Oklahoma Compensation Division, *Oklahoma Merit System Classification and Compensation Plan* (Oklahoma City, OK: State of Oklahoma Compensation Division, 1996).

23. Pennsylvania League of Cities and Municipalities, *1996 Salary and Benefits Survey* (Harrisburg, PA: Pennsylvania League of Cities and Municipalities, 1996).

24. Technical Assistance Center, *1988 National Nonprofit Wage & Benefits Survey* (Denver, CO: Technical Assistance Center, 1988).

25. Texas Municipal League, *1996 Salaries and Fringe Benefits of Texas City Officials* (Austin, TX: Texas Municipal League, 1996).

26. Towers Perrin, *Compensation Survey of Management Positions in High-Technology Companies* (Rosslyn, VA: Towers Perrin, 1995).

27. Towers Perrin, *1996 Management Compensation Report, Not-for-Profit Organizations* (Rosslyn, VA: Towers Perrin, 1996).

28. U.S. Department of Labor, "Occupational Compensation Survey, National Summary, 1994," Bulletin 2479 (Washington, DC: U.S. Department of Labor, 1996).

29. U.S. Department of Labor, "Occupational Compensation Survey:

Pay and Benefits," *Bulletin 3085-1* (Denver, CO: U.S. Department of Labor, 1996).

30. U.S. Department of Labor, "Occupational Compensation Survey: Pay Only West Palm Beach," *Bulletin 3085-10* (Boca Raton, FL: U.S. Department of Labor, 1996).

31. U.S. Department of Labor, "Employee Benefits in Medium and Large Private Establishments, 1993," *Bulletin 2456* (Washington, DC: U.S. Department of Labor, 1994).

32. U.S. Department of Labor, "Employee Benefits in Small Private Establishments, 1994," *Bulletin 2475* (Washington, DC: U.S. Department of Labor, 1996).

33. U.S. Department of Labor, "Employee Benefits Survey: A BLS Reader," *Bulletin 2459* (Washington, DC: U.S. Department of Labor, 1995).

34. U.S. Department of Labor, "Employee Benefits in State and Local Governments, 1994," *Bulletin 2477* (Washington, DC: U.S. Department of Labor, 1996).

35. William M. Mercer, Inc., 1996, "What the Rest of Us Make," *Mercury News* (On-line). Available: http://www.sjmercury.com.

CHAPTER FIVE

Innovative Compensation Practices in the Nonprofit Sector

THE NEED FOR INFORMATION ON INNOVATIVE COMPENSATION PRACTICES

ARDI's 1990 cross-sector compensation study demonstrated that nonprofits were in a poor competitive position relative to other sectors regarding compensation and motivational employment practices. Despite the increased interest in nonprofit compensation, the current 1996 cross-sector comparison data shows that the nonprofit sector still lags behind the for-profit and government sectors in offering competitive compensation packages to employees. However, the 1996 data and the results of a 1995 ARDI study on innovative compensation practices show that nonprofit organizations are increasingly incorporating such practices in their efforts to recruit and retain qualified personnel.

Incentive plans, cash and noncash recognition, and other innovative compensation and human resource practices are becoming critical elements in the organizational strategy of many nonprofit organizations. ARDI conducted a study in 1994 and published the results in a 1995 book *Innovative Compensation Practices in the Nonprofit Sector* (2). This study analyzed a sample of innovative compensation programs, learned how they affected nonprofit organizations, and broadened the information base available to the nonprofit sector on this management topic. Information and data on innovative compensation practices in the nonprofit sector are not regularly reported in surveys, and ARDI was unable to include any significant survey data on this topic in the cross-sector comparison analysis. Therefore, this section includes information from the 1995 publication in order to provide nonprofit organizations with compensation options other than standard wage-and-benefit practices.

METHODOLOGY OF STUDY ON INNOVATIVE COMPENSATION PRACTICES

In preparation for conducting its study on innovative compensation practices, ARDI recruited an Advisory Committee for the project, consisting of five compensation experts and sector leaders with expertise in human resource management of nonprofits. The role of the Advisory Committee was to identify topics to be included, to identify references, to provide guidance on the study process, to assist in identifying nonprofit organizations likely to have instituted innovative compensation programs, to provide analysis and advice as the study progressed, to review the report prior to publication, and to assist in the dissemination of results.

Reference materials were reviewed and analyzed for trends in innovative compensation practice programs and environmental factors related to the use of such programs. Standard terminology related to general innovative compensation practices was clarified and modified for inclusion in the study. Definitions of specific types of programs are provided later in this section.

A letter and brief initial survey questionnaire were sent to 182 potential nonprofit participants identified as good prospects for having implemented an innovative compensation program. A total of 43 nonprofit organizations responded to the initial survey questionnaire. This represented a response rate of 24 percent of the 182 nonprofits invited to participate. After screening the responses to the initial survey questionnaire, a second more comprehensive and confidential questionnaire was designed. This eleven-page questionnaire included detailed questions on each type of innovative compensation program. Of the 43 responses to the initial survey, ARDI screened out 12 nonprofits that did not have innovative compensation or benefits programs. Thus, 31 nonprofit organizations were invited to participate in the second survey, based on the types of cash compensation and/or benefit programs they implemented. A total of 18 nonprofits completed and returned the second survey questionnaire. The survey results were then analyzed, and the findings are also presented later in this section.

Phone interviews were conducted with selected final-survey participants to obtain both further insights into the operation of their plans and their perceptions and prognosis for the future. In addition, the telephone calls included clarification of survey responses provided by participants and obtained additional data when necessary.

A Preliminary Report was drafted for review and input by the Advisory Committee and revised to incorporate their comments. The Final Report was developed for review by the Advisory Committee and then published by ARDI.

DEFINITIONS

Innovative compensation practices encompass cash-compensation, recognition, and benefit plan options. The following definitions include nine examples of innovative cash-compensation or recognition plan options and six examples of innovative benefit options that were studied.

Cash-Compensation or Recognition Plans

Individual incentives—Cash awards to recognize achievement of *predetermined performance objectives*. An incentive award is usually calculated as a percentage of salary or salary-range midpoint and is paid on an annual basis. Incentive awards are usually larger than spot awards and are frequently used at the managerial level.

Team or group incentives—Same as individual incentives, except awards are made based on achievement of team or group predetermined performance objectives. (Based on the research conducted in association with this study, these types of awards do not appear to be commonly found in nonprofits.)

Bonuses—Awards paid at senior management's discretion to acknowledge outstanding individual job performance or to encourage special activities. Bonuses are usually paid at the managerial level; unlike an incentive award, the amount of a bonus is discretionary because it is not based on a predetermined formula.

Gain sharing—Awards that represent employees' share of the gains of actual results achieved above preestablished operational goals. The "gains" are paid in the form of short-term cash incentive awards when the goals are exceeded. Traditional plans often focus on *productivity goals* such as costs in each unit of production or labor hours per unit of production for *nonmanagerial operating employees in manufacturing*. More recent plans include broader objectives in the formula, such as quality, customer service, and responsiveness. (Based on the research conducted in association with this study, such plans are very rare in nonprofit organizations, and their potential application for nonprofits seems limited.)

Spot awards—Cash payments to provide *immediate recognition* of accomplishments by staff below the managerial level. They are intended to reward risk taking, creativity, and productivity. Awards are usually paid immediately after the accomplishment and are separate from the regular salary administration program. Spot awards may be used to recognize either individual or team achievements. *Awards are generally smaller than bonuses and typically range from $250 to $500.*

Special cash recognition—Similar to a spot award program, these are cash awards used to recognize contributions of staff below a certain managerial level. Awards are granted on a discretionary basis to employees who demonstrate either a sustained level of exceptional performance or exceptional performance on one program or project. *Awards typically range from $500 to $1,000 and are paid quarterly.*

Special noncash recognition—Noncash awards used to recognize contributions of staff below a certain managerial level. Awards are not paid in cash, but in the form of merchandise, a gift certificate, an evening out, and so on.

Lump sum increases—Cash payments usually made in a single lump sum for performance effectiveness. They do not roll into base salary. Another variation is to spread out payment over several pay periods. Awards are sometimes used only for employees above salary-range midpoint or at/over salary-range maximum. They replace a more traditional merit increase that is paid out in the form of an adjustment to base pay.

Skill-based pay—Pay based on acquiring additional job-related skills and capabilities. Also known as *pay for knowledge*, this option is traditionally used for teachers, scientists, and accountants. A number of organizations now use skill-based pay for hourly, nonexempt employees. Pay structure consists of a starting rate and several higher pay levels, each defined by a set of competencies known as "skill blocks." The salary-range spread may be 80 percent from the lowest to highest rate.

Benefit Plans

Day care provisions—Includes on- or off-site facilities or reimbursement for day care expenses for employees' children.

Dependent care—Plan allows qualifying dependent care expenses to be paid by employees on a pretax basis.

Flexible spending accounts—Also called *reimbursement accounts*, this option provides employer funds, employee pretax money, or both to be used for expenses typically not covered by the benefits package. Typical expenses that may be reimbursed include health care coinsurance, deductibles, and other out-of-pocket health expenses; insurance premiums; and child care costs. Reimbursement accounts may be part of a flexible benefits plan, or they may stand alone.

Flextime/staggered hours—Provides employees with flexibility in setting their work schedules. Employees can choose the time they wish to begin work, and their ending time relates accordingly.

Job-sharing—Allows two or more part-time employees to perform the responsibilities of one full-time job. The employees' salaries are usually prorated, based on hours worked. Benefits may also be prorated or not offered. This arrangement may be beneficial for employees who do not wish to work full-time but whose experience may be valuable to the employer.

Premium conversion plan—Allows employees to pay health insurance premiums on a pretax basis.

ANALYSIS AND FINDINGS

Two surveys were conducted during the course of the study's research process in 1994. The objective of the surveys was to gather information on innovative compensation plans in effect at a sampling of nonprofit organizations. The first survey was designed to identify organizations with plans in place. The second survey was designed to gather detailed information about those existing plans.

Participant Profile

The Advisory Committee assisted in identifying the 182 nonprofits invited to participate in the initial survey. These organizations were considered likely to have an innovative compensation program in place. There were 43 replies to the initial survey, which represents a 24 percent response rate. Of the 43 replies, 12 organizations did not have innovative compensation plans in place and, therefore, were excluded from the second survey. ARDI then invited the 31 nonprofits that had a variety of innovative programs to participate in the second survey. Eighteen of the 31 organizations actually completed and returned the second, comprehensive survey questionnaire, for a 58 percent response rate.

While the response represented a select sample of nonprofits, it does provide current information on organizations with innovative compensation programs. It should be noted that all 18 participants did not respond to every question, which is not unusual with a comprehensive survey of this type. Therefore, the survey results reported reflect only those organizations responding to a given question.

All 18 participants had the 501(c)(3) nonprofit designation. The 18 nonprofit organizations that participated in the innovative compensation study provide a variety of services, as illustrated in Exhibit 5.1.

The innovative compensation plans in the participating nonprofit organizations covered staff in a variety of locations. One organization had hundreds of locations in all regions of the United States and internationally. The remaining nonprofit participants have thirty-two locations in the geographic areas shown in Exhibit 5.2.

Of the 18 nonprofit organizations reporting numbers of employees, 14 have less than 100 employees. Three organizations have between 101 and 400 employees. One international organization has approximately 17,000 employees. Exhibit 5.3 summarizes employment for the participating nonprofits. The median employment was thirty-four people, excluding the largest organization because it is an anomaly in terms of size.

Exhibit 5.1   Participant Profile

Major Groups*	Number	Percent
Arts and Culture	1	6%
Human Services	10	55%
Health/Mental Health, Crisis Intervention	1	6%
Education/Instruction Related, Information and		
Nonformal	5	27%
Community Improvement/Capacity Building	1	6%
TOTAL	18	100%

Source: *National Taxonomy of Exempt Entities, "Mapping the Nonprofit Sector," National Center for Charitable Statistics: A Program of Independent Sector (1).

Exhibit 5.2   Geographic Areas Represented by Participants

Areas of United States	No. of Locations	% of Total
Northeast (ME, VT, NH, CT, RI, MA, NY, NJ, PA)	8	25%
Midwest (OH, IN, IL, MI, WI)	9	28%
North Central (MN, IA, MO, ND, SD, NE, KS)	7	22%
South (KY, TN, AL, MS, DE, MD, DC, VA, WV, NC,		
SC, GA, FL, PR)	4	13%
Southwest (AR, LA, OK, TX)	1	3%
Mountain (MT, ID, WY, CO, NM, AZ, UT, NV)	1	3%
Pacific (WA, OR, CA, AK, HI, GU)	2	6%
TOTAL LOCATIONS	32	100%

Exhibit 5.3   Number of Employees

Total No. of Employees	No. of Nonprofits Surveyed
0–10	2
11–25	4
26–50	7
51–100	1
101–400	3
~17,000	1

General Plan Information

This section provides an overview of ARDI's findings on the following topics: eligibility for innovative compensation plans; number of survey participants implementing such plans within the past several years; objectives organizations were trying to achieve by implementing these types of innovative programs; "champion" of the new plans; length of design process; and required approvals.

Eligibility for Innovative Compensation Plans

Fourteen of the 18 nonprofits reporting data indicated that their entire employee population was eligible for their innovative compensation plans. Of the organizations with some limits on their employees' participation in such innovative plans, only one excluded nonexempt employees.

Number of Survey Participants Implementing Such Plans

Eleven of the 18 nonprofits have implemented both innovative cash compensation or recognition and benefit plans. Thirteen of the 18 nonprofits introduced innovative cash compensation plans. Of these 13 organizations, all but two implemented the compensation program since 1991. Innovative benefit programs were established by 16 of the 18 nonprofits. All except one of these 16 organizations established their innovative benefit plans since 1989.

Objectives That Organizations Were Trying to Achieve by Implementing These Types of Innovative Programs

A key factor for success was defining the objectives to be achieved by implementing an innovative compensation benefit program. All 18 nonprofits indicated multiple reasons for creating new programs. More than half of the participants indicated that their program objectives included the following:

- Improve morale and/or employee relations
- Improve employee retention
- Link pay to performance/improve employee performance
- Become more competitive in total compensation (i.e., compensation and benefits)

Approximately one quarter of the survey respondents described the objectives that their organizations were trying to achieve by installing the programs as follows:

- Assist in recruiting
- Reduce entitlement mentality
- Reinforce an existing environment of participation
- Foster teamwork
- Upgrade quality of workforce

Exhibit 5.4 cites the number of participants indicating specific program objectives.

"Champion" of the New Plans

The mandate to introduce innovative compensation plans came from top management. Fourteen of the 18 participants indicated

Exhibit 5.4   Program Objectives

top management was the initial "champion" or "sponsor" for this change. There was no clear-cut consensus on the composition of the plan-design committee. The most frequent response was that the executive director and/or senior management and human resources participated in the plan-design committee. This is not unusual because there are several smaller nonprofits included in the survey sample.

Length of Design Process

The design process ranged from one week to twenty-six weeks, from the beginning of the plan-design process to the plan's introduction. The most typical time frame was six to eight weeks. Management usually selected the task force members, and others were volunteers or members of board committees.

Required Approvals

Top management approval was necessary for plan implementation in 17 of the 18 participating organizations. The compensation committee and/or the board of directors required additional approval in 8 of the 18 nonprofits.

Innovative Cash Compensation or Recognition Plans

Overview of Survey Results

The following information focuses exclusively on cash compensation or recognition plans. Innovative benefit plans are reviewed in detail later in this section. An overview of the survey results regarding cash compensation and/or recognition plans is provided here. The most popular types of compensation programs implemented by the participants were bonuses, incentives, and noncash recognition programs. The majority of the nonprofits that had implemented such programs had at least two types of cash compensation and/or recognition programs. Management set specific guidelines concerning the design of the innovative compensation or recognition programs, including identifying the plan objectives. The compensation plan's objectives were linked to the nonprofit's long-term objectives.

Seven of the 13 respondents used a flat dollar amount as the form of award payout for the compensation plan. Five of the 13 respondents used a percentage of salary for the award payout, and target payouts typically ranged from 2 percent to 5 percent of salary. Cash was used as the most prevalent form of award payout, and the awards were often paid separately from regular paychecks.

The performance criteria most often used in the innovative compensation programs were productivity, financial, and quality measures. Management usually set the plan's baseline according to the organization's historical performance alone or in combination with other factors. Top management often handled the administration of the innovative compensation plan alone or in conjunction with others, such as the human resources department, board of directors, or volunteer committee.

Top management usually communicated information regarding the innovative compensation plan. The sharing of information with participants concerning frequency and performance of the plan payouts was handled in a variety of ways. Information was usually communicated each time awards were paid because the payout was indicative of performance level. Nonprofits used a combination of methods to communicate information, including newsletters, memos, and meetings. The communications with plan participants generally included only compensation plan payout or information related to performance on payout, award measures, and payout amount. Seven of the respondents reported the frequency of communications between management and plan participants remained about the same as before the innovative compensation plan was created. Five of the respondents reported more frequent communications than before the plan was implemented.

All 13 organizations that had implemented innovative compensation cash or recognition programs reported their plans had been successful. They reported a total of fifty-five positive results, ranging from three to eleven per nonprofit organization. As a result of the implementation of the innovative compensation plan, ten of the respondents indicated some improvement in employee involvement in problem solving and/or decision making in their organizational unit.

Types of Innovative Cash Compensation Programs Implemented

A total of twenty-eight types of innovative compensation and/ or recognition plans were implemented by 13 of the 18 survey participants. Bonuses, incentives, and noncash recognition programs were the most prevalent types of innovative compensation programs established. Other types of programs implemented among the nonprofit participants included team/group incentives, spot awards, cash recognition, and lump-sum merit. The majority of the nonprofits that had implemented such programs had used at least two types of cash compensation and recognition programs. Exhibit 5.5 describes the variety of cash compensation and/or recognition plans established by the nonprofit organizations surveyed.

Exhibit 5.5 Types of Innovative Cash Compensation Programs Implemented

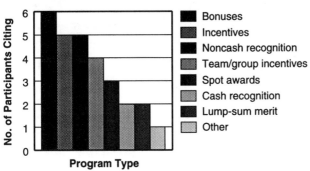

Implications for the Design of Innovative
Cash Compensation Programs

The program types mentioned in Exhibit 5.5 require guidelines set by management in the design of the innovative compensation programs. The most frequently cited guidelines included the following:

- Eligible employee group
- Expected or minimum level of organizational performance
- Plan objectives
- Performance measures
- Form of award payout (cash or equivalent)
- Budget for maximum payouts

According to the survey results, the innovative compensation plan objectives had a moderate to strong connection to the organization's long-term objectives in 12 of the 13 responding survey participants.

Teamwork and Collaboration

Eleven of the 18 survey participants indicated that groups or individuals do not compete with one another for award payouts.

Time between End of Plan Period and Payout

The average length of time between end of measured plan period and payout ranges from one to four weeks for spot awards, noncash incentives, and team incentives. For bonuses and incentives, the average time frame is much longer, ranging from two weeks to one year.

Plan Payouts as Percentage of Payroll

Five of the 10 respondents that reported information on payouts indicated their innovative compensation plan payouts were less than 1.5 percent of total payroll. About one-third of the respondents reported their plan awards ranged between 3 percent and 6 percent of total payroll.

Innovative Cash Compensation Plan as Substitute for Other Compensation Elements

Of the 7 nonprofits indicating their innovative compensation plan was a substitute for other compensation elements, 5 reported it represented a replacement for future base-salary increases. One organization also reported it froze base-pay levels.

Basis Used for Form of Compensation Award Payout

Of the 12 nonprofits that reported on the form of award payout for their compensation plan, 4 used a flat dollar amount, and 2 used a percent of salary. Five used a combination of length of service and a flat dollar amount or a percentage of salary. One organization used elements other than those just cited. Exhibit 5.6 displays this information.

Target Award Payouts

Eight of the 18 survey participants indicated targeted average payouts for individual awards. The target payouts typically ranged from 2 percent to 5 percent of salary. In one organization,

Exhibit 5.6   Form of Award Payout

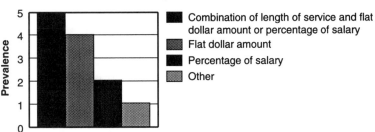

targeted payout ranged form 4 percent to 10 percent of salary-range midpoint. A small number of nonprofits indicated flat dollar amounts, such as $50 to $250 for spot awards and $250 for cash recognition awards. Less than half of the respondents indicated their innovative compensation plans included a maximum individual payout.

Cash/Noncash as Form of Award Payout

Not surprisingly, cash was the most prevalent form of payout used for the innovative compensation plan awards. Eight of the 13 participants responding indicated their award payouts were made 100 percent in cash. Three of the participants paid between 95 percent and 99 percent of the award in cash, with the remainder in noncash and/or time off. One organization paid 60 percent in cash, and the remaining 40 percent was evenly divided into symbolic recognition and merchandise. One organization used time off or special luncheons, rather than cash, for their awards. Exhibit 5.7 displays this information.

Award Payout as Separate Check

In 8 of the 11 organizations responding to this question, employees received their compensation plan awards separately from their regular paychecks, especially if it represented a bonus payout. The remaining 3 organizations included spot awards and/or team incentives in employees' regular paychecks.

Exhibit 5.7   Cash/NonCash as Form of Award Payout

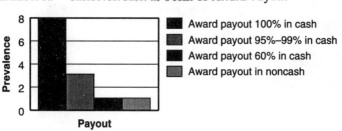

Performance Criteria for Compensation Plans

Productivity, financial, and quality measures were the performance criteria most often used as the basis for the respondents'
compensation awards under a variety of programs. The combination of productivity and quality was cited for awards in bonus, spot award, cash recognition, and lump-sum merit increase
payments.

Baseline Used for Innovative Compensation Plans

The innovative compensation plan's baseline was established
based on historical performance alone or in addition to other
factors in more than half of the 11 respondents. Management set
the plan's baseline or goal for 8 of the 11 organizations responding—for at least one type of compensation program. The 10 respondents who described how they adjusted the baseline or goal
from one plan period to another were almost equally divided
among the following:

- Baseline does not change—4
- Previous plan-period performance becomes the new
  baseline—3
- Other (e.g., availability of funds)—3

Administration of Compensation Plan

The administration of the innovative compensation plan was
usually handled by top management alone or in conjunction with
others in 8 of the 13 respondents (see Exhibit 5.8). The human
resources department alone handled the plan's administration in
4 of the 13 organizations. In one organization, a volunteer committee handled the plan's administration.

Communications with Compensation Plan Participants

Top management in 8 of the 12 responding nonprofits communicated information regarding innovative compensation plans. The

Exhibit 5.8   Cash Compensation Plan Administration

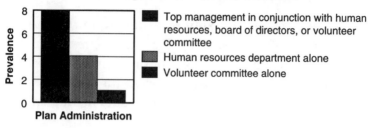

4 remaining organizations each used one primary source to communicate plan information; they were: organizational unit management, human resources, immediate supervisor, and a combination of two of the primary sources just cited.

The sharing of information with plan participants concerning frequency and performance of innovative compensation plan payouts or award measures was handled in a variety of ways. Of the 12 organizations supplying responses, 7 provided information each time awards were paid because payout indicated performance level. Meetings were used by 5 organizations to share information with plan participants. Four of these 5 organizations used a combination of methods, including newsletters or memos and organizational, departmental, or work-group meetings in their communications campaigns.

The amount of detail included in these communications follows:

- Payout amount only—5
- Performance on payout, award measures, and payout amount—5
- Previous two items, plus management's comments—2

Changes in Frequency of Communications as a Result of Compensation Plan

The survey participants were asked whether the frequency of communications between management and plan participants had changed as a result of the innovative compensation plan. Eleven participants replied, and 7 of those reported the frequency of communication was the same as before the plan was created. The remaining 4 organizations responded that the frequency improved since the plan was implemented.

Changes in Employee Involvement in Problem Solving and/or Decision Making as a Result of the Compensation Plan

The nonprofit participants were queried as to the degree that the innovative compensation plan encouraged employee involvement in organizational-unit problem solving and/or decision making. Ten of the 13 organizations responding reported some degree of encouragement, usually rated as moderate or slightly higher. Only 3 of the 13 organizations reported no change because employee involvement had already existed.

Positive Results of Implementing Innovative Cash Compensation or Recognition Plans

1. The 13 nonprofit organizations that had innovative compensation plans all reported success.
2. Seven of the responding nonprofits reported the following positive results:
   - Linking pay to performance improved employee performance
   - Improved employee morale and/or employee relations
   - Fostered teamwork
3. Additional positive results mentioned by various survey participants included:
   - Enhanced communication of unit goals
   - Reinforced an existing or created a participative environment
   - Improved employee retention

- Reduced entitlement mentality
- Made labor costs vary with organizational performance
- Became more competitive in total compensation
- Encouraged entrepreneurship
- Assisted in recruiting

Exhibit 5.9 depicts the positive results achieved. The 13 nonprofits with successful compensation plans reported a total of 55 positive results, ranging from three to eleven per organization.

It is the authors' collective experience that employees appreciate being recognized for their contributions to the organization. This is especially true when the recognition is in a tangible form, such as cash. When the recognition is in a noncash form, employees like being acknowledged by their peers and supervisors. The recognition enhances their sense of teamwork and contribution to the organization's success. Innovative compensation plans tend to add more focus and communication to the organization's overall goals. This increased communication helps create a more participative environment and reduces an entitlement mentality. When an organization's total compensation becomes more competitive, this factor can help improve employee retention.

Exhibit 5.9   Positive Results Achieved as a Result of Implementing Innovative Compensation Plans

Results	Frequency
Improved employee performance	10
Improved morale and/or employee relations	8
Fostered teamwork	7
Enhanced communication of unit goals	6
Reinforced an existing environment of participation	4
Improved employee retention	4
Created a participative environment	3
Reduced entitlement mentality	3
Made labor costs variable with organizational performance	3
Became more competitive in total compensation	3
Encouraged entrepreneurship	2
Assisted in recruiting	1

Issues as a Result of Implementing Innovative Cash Compensation and Recognition Plans

Three of the 4 organizations reporting some issues indicated they experienced administrative/operational concerns that required continued attention as a result of implementing their innovative compensation plans. Some specific examples include:

- Some negative employee-relations impact due to awards paid only to managerial level
- Difficulty of defining performance objectives for the overall organization and individual plan participants, particularly qualitative performance objectives
- The potential emphasis on short-term objectives at the expense of the long-term goals of the organization
- The discomfort expressed by some long-term employees of nonprofits who are more comfortable with traditional compensation practices under which their pay is not at risk.

Notwithstanding, these organizations all rated their plans as successful.

There are some caveats that nonprofit organizations considering the use of innovative compensation plans, particularly incentives, should keep in mind. The types of questions most frequently encountered usually are related to the following issues:

Participation—How to establish plan eligibility and determine the criteria for inclusion in the plan. The most frequently used criteria are grade level or position in the organization's hierarchy.

Funding—In a self-funding plan, it is useful to establish a threshold, which activates the plan, based on overall organizational performance; for example, an organization fundraising goal of 3 percent must be realized.

Definition of goal levels—Specific definition of goals can prevent potential manipulation of the plan.

Qualitative goals—Performance objectives should include both quantitative and qualitative goals. The qualitative goals could include the level of service, productivity, and specific projects. Because these goals may be difficult to quantify, they require well-defined narrative descriptions of goal minimums, targets, and maximums.

Unexpected occurrences—There may be certain significant events, both positive and negative, that are out of employees' control and that may impact the plan's potential payouts. The plan should be flexible enough to allow for such unplanned occurrences, without penalizing the plan participants (3).

In addition to the caveats just described, it is important for nonprofit organizations to be aware of the risks of a poorly designed incentive plan, for it may not produce the expected results. Examples of such risks include the following:

Perceived favoritism—A totally discretionary plan, with award payouts made exclusively on the basis of subjective judgments, rather than well-defined performance measures, might be viewed by the participants as being arbitrary or based on favoritism. This could be counter-productive to the organization as it may alienate those employees the plan was created to reward.

Performance measures should be realistic. They should not be so easy that the participants can achieve their objectives without much effort, nor so difficult that they are unreasonable.

There should not be an overemphasis on short-term achievements, such as raising funds or increasing revenues, at the expense of the organization's long-term goals. To guard against this risk, it is important to keep the organization's primary mission in mind when choosing performance measures. The goals, goal levels, and their definitions should be reviewed annually to ensure changing priorities are incorporated into the plan design (3).

It may be wise to retain a compensation consultant if such expertise does not exist on staff. Further, a review of the plan before finalization by a lawyer with appropriate expertise is also recommended.

Innovative Benefit Plans

Overview of Survey Results

The following information focuses exclusively on benefit plans, just as cash compensation or recognition plans were reviewed earlier in this section. An overview of the survey results regarding benefit plans is provided here. The most popular types of benefit programs implemented by the participants were flextime/ staggered hours, flexible spending accounts, and dependent care. Other types of programs introduced included premium conversion, day care, and job-sharing. Thirteen of the 16 nonprofits that had implemented such programs had at least two types of benefit programs.

The human resources departments most frequently handled the administration of the innovative benefit plans. Top management and the finance department were also cited by some nonprofits as responsible for the benefit plan's administration; still other organizations used a combination of two of these three sources to administer their benefit plans.

The human resources department was often responsible for communications related to the organization's benefit plans. Some nonprofits used a combination of two or three areas, including top management, organizational-unit management, human resources, immediate supervisor, or plan administrator, to handle benefit-plan communications with employees. The sharing of information with benefit-plan participants was usually communicated through meetings or a combination of meetings and newsletters or memos. Nine of the 16 respondents reported that the frequency of communications between management and benefit-plan participants remained about the same as before the innovative benefit plan was created; 6 organizations replied that the frequency was somewhat improved, and 1 organization reported that the frequency had definitely increased.

Fifteen of the 16 nonprofits responding reported that their innovative benefit plans had been successfully implemented. One organization reported it was too soon to judge because its new plan had been in place for less than a year. The 16 organizations that reported successful implementation of their benefit plans cited a total of forty-nine positive results, ranging from two to five per nonprofit organization. Fifteen of the 16 respondents reported at least one, and in most cases several, of the following positive results:

- Improved morale and/or employee relations
- Improved employee retention
- More competitive total compensation
- Improved recruiting

Additional positive results included upgraded quality of workforce and enhanced communication of objectives.

Types of Innovative Benefit Plans

The 16 responding survey participants offer a variety of innovative benefit plans (see Exhibit 5.10) ranging from one to five types of plans per organization. The most popular benefit programs offered were flextime/staggered hours and flexible spending accounts. Flextime was highly valued by employees because it provided flexibility to accommodate personal needs. Flextime/staggered hours were offered at little or no cost to the organization. It usually involved coordination of schedules to insure work coverage for beginning and ending work hours. Flexible spending accounts, also known as reimbursement accounts, were quite popular. They provided employer funds, employee pretax money, or both to be used for expenses typically not covered by the benefits package. Typical expenses that may be reimbursed include health care coinsurance, deductibles, out-of-pocket health

Exhibit 5.10   Types of Innovative Benefit Plans Offered in the Nonprofits
Surveyed

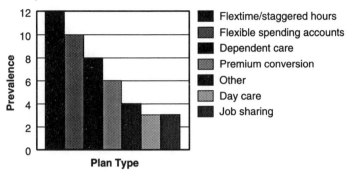

expenses, insurance premiums, and child care costs. Reimbursement accounts may be part of a flexible benefits plan, or they may
stand alone. Dependent care was another popular benefit, and
reimbursement for such care from pretax dollars was sometimes
offered as a choice under a flexible spending account.

Administration of Benefit Plans

Human resources was most frequently cited as the department
responsible for the benefit plan administration. Some nonprofits
had top management or the finance department take care of the
administration of the benefit plans. Other nonprofits used a combination of two of the three areas cited to handle the benefit-plan
administration. Exhibit 5.11 illustrates the various ways the 16
respondents handled the administration of such plans.

Exhibit 5.11   Benefit-Plan Administration

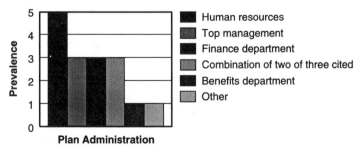

Methods Used to Communicate Information Regarding the Benefit Plan

The nonprofits reported a variety of methods used to communicate information regarding the innovative benefit plans. This information was usually communicated through meetings, including organizational, unit, departmental, or work group, or a combination of meetings and newsletters or memos. Exhibit 5.12 indicates the methods used by the 16 respondents to communicate information about their benefit plans.

Communications with Benefit-Plan Participants

Communications about the organization's benefit plans were often handled by human resources. Some nonprofits used a combination of two or three areas, including top management, organizational-unit management, human resources, immediate supervisor, or plan administrator. Exhibit 5.13 describes the primary responsibility for benefit-plan communications.

Changes in Frequency of Communications as a Result of Benefit Plan

The participating nonprofits were queried regarding whether the frequency of plan communications had changed due to the implementation of the innovative benefit plans. Sixteen participants replied, and 9 of those reported that the frequency of communications between management and plan participants was the same

Exhibit 5.12   Communication Methods

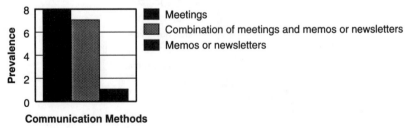

Meetings
Combination of meetings and memos or newsletters
Memos or newsletters

Prevalence

Communication Methods

Exhibit 5.13   Communication Responsibility

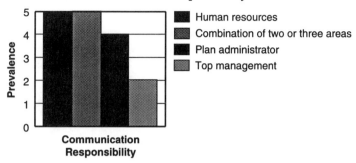

as before the benefit plan was created. Six responded that the frequency had increased somewhat from what it was before the benefit plan was in use. The 1 remaining organization reported that the frequency of communications had definitely increased as a result of the innovative benefit plan.

Positive Results of Implementing Innovative Benefit Plan(s)

Of the 16 nonprofits that offered innovative benefit plans, 15 reported that their plans had been implemented successfully. The remaining organization replied that it was too soon to know because its new plan had been in place for less than a year. Of the 16 nonprofits who responded, 15 reported positive results, including improved morale and/or employee relations. There were 11 organizations that indicated an improvement in employee retention. Because benefits are considered an indirect form of total compensation, the innovative benefit plans were perceived as increasing the organization's competitive position. They were considered as another tool in recruiting staff to the nonprofits. The 16 organizations that reported that their benefit plans were successful reported a total of 49 positive results, ranging from two to five per organization. Details about the positive results achieved as a result of establishing their innovative benefit plans are shown in Exhibit 5.14.

Exhibit 5.14 Positive Results Achieved as a Result of Establishing Innovative Benefit Plans

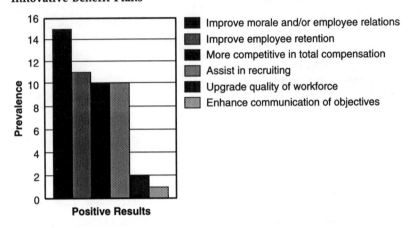

Issues as a Result of Implementing Innovative Benefit Plans

Five organizations reported some issues requiring attention as a result of implementing their innovative benefit plans. Three of the 5 organizations experienced some administrative issues. Some of the specific issues described included revisions needed for the technical details of the benefits plans, clarification of spending accounts and other insurance options, and IRS reporting requirements.

Based on the authors' experience, organizations that may be considering innovative benefit plans should develop detailed administrative procedures during the plan-design stages. A manual of clearly defined administrative procedures would minimize potential issues and assist in the plan's smooth implementation.

Nonprofit organizations considering innovative benefit plans should be aware that there are certain caveats related to such plans. In the authors' experience, such caveats include the following:

Board Responsibilities and Employee Involvement—The board is ultimately responsible for establishing the compensation policies, including determining what innovative compensation programs the organization will employ and if they will be employed. As such the board must be involved, either through committee work or, in the case of a small board, acting as a committee of the whole on the matter, in studying and establishing all compensation policies and overseeing their equitable implementation. They will want to delegate information preparation to the executive and gain input from supervisors and employees on what outcomes are to be achieved by the innovative and all compensation plan elements. They may wish to obtain employee reaction to proposed new aspects of the compensation package. Creating such input mechanisms helps to ensure the fit of compensation practices to employee needs and desires and creates "buy in" and/or identifies potential problems that can then be addressed in implementation planning. Employees must be educated before they can choose wisely among an indemnity plan, preferred provider network, health maintenance organization, and so on. It may take a while for employees to adjust to the new programs, and individual employees or groups of like employees may react differently to elements of the plan.

Potential Costs—The cost of hiring a benefits consultant to provide advice on how to approach this issue can be substantial. There may be several one-time expenses, such as an employee survey to identify how the staff would react to different types of innovative benefit plans; communications materials and meetings to announce the new plans; costs related to determining whether change in insurance carriers is appropriate; and computer programming and set-up charges for handling benefits administration.

Because benefits plans are governed by a variety of regulations, as well as IRS reporting requirements, hiring a consultant or a lawyer who specializes in benefits may be a wise investment. Unless the nonprofit has a benefits professional on staff who is very knowledgeable in this area, it could be a costly mistake not to hire a consultant or a lawyer to design and implement an innovative benefit plan.

Time—The authors' experience has been that an innovative benefit plan can take at least a year from the planning and design stage to the implementation stage, based on the extent of the plan revisions. This process can take an enormous amount of staff time as the nonprofit handles this process alone or with a consultant or lawyer. Until the new plan is implemented, the nonprofit might consider arranging a temporary transfer of day-to-day tasks for the staff person charged with handling this project.

Communications—A variety of clear and frequent communications to employees about changes to benefit plans is important. Simple and well-written benefit materials should be distributed to all employees. Meetings should also be held to inform employees of the changes and to provide them with the opportunity to ask questions. Changes in the benefit plan will have an impact on employees and their families, especially if their dependents are covered.

CASE STUDIES

The following four case studies will illustrate the way that three nonprofit organizations and a composite of several nonprofit organizations approached instituting an innovative compensation program. The composite case study consists of input from several nonprofit organizations that reported on their results in implementing a noncash recognition plan.

Case Study 1: Management Incentive Plan

Background

This nonprofit, with less than 100 employees, wished to enhance its strategic planning process, to improve efficiency levels, and to stimulate productivity within the organization. The organization determined that the people most able to control and impact the organization's strategic goals were its senior managers. An incentive compensation plan was viewed as a tool to attract, retain, and motivate senior managers. Accordingly, the executive director and the senior officers who reported to the executive director were identified as those eligible to participate in the management incentive compensation plan.

The incentive plan was implemented to reward senior managers for achieving or exceeding the organization's objectives, as well as their own individual performance objectives. The plan linked the level of award payments to actual achievement of the following types of objectives: significant increases in income, broader community organization and program objectives, and development of more sophisticated financial systems and procedures.

One of the goals of the plan was to change the makeup of each senior manager's total cash-compensation package by adding a variable component (pay at risk) in the form of an incentive award, while slowing the growth of the senior managers' base salary (fixed compensation costs) with modest annual general or cost-of-living increases to salary. Therefore, for the employee, total cash-compensation levels were expected to remain competitive with the marketplace if targeted performance objectives were achieved. The organization, on the other hand, would achieve better control of compensation costs by paying out only if organizational performance objectives were achieved. In addition, the incentive plan was designed to insure that compensation costs under the incentive plan and the traditional merit increase plan were equivalent at the *target* (or expected) level of manager performance.

The incentive plan offered the opportunity to earn annual awards amounting to as much as 15 percent of the salary-range midpoint at the maximum ("far exceeds standards") level of performance. At the threshold ("meets standard") level, the award payouts equaled 5 percent of the salary-range midpoint; and at the target ("exceeds standard") level, the awards equaled 10 percent of the range midpoint. All awards were contingent on meeting predetermined organizational and individual performance objectives.

This nonprofit organization was interested in reinforcing its culture of teamwork among senior management and in increasing their overall focus on the organization's strategic goals. Accordingly, the incentive compensation plan took both of these factors into account in determining the total potential awards. For the senior officers reporting to the executive director, the incentive awards were based 50 percent on achievement of organizational objectives (e.g., fund-raising growth/control of fund-raising costs, net income growth, program service and delivery goals, and financial administration) and 50 percent on individual and departmental objectives. For the executive director, the percentages were 80 percent for the organizational objectives and 20 percent for the individual objectives.

The executive director was responsible for reviewing and evaluating the actual achievement of performance objectives of the senior officers as soon as financial and other year-end reports were available. The executive director's performance was reviewed and evaluated by the compensation committee of the board of directors. All incentive compensation-plan awards were subject to final review and approval by the compensation committee, with final approval by the board of directors.

Summary of Management Incentive Plan Elements

- Eligibility: Executive director and senior officers reporting to executive director
- Plan purposes:
  1. Attract, retain, and motivate senior officers to higher performance levels
  2. Change mix of compensation elements by adding a variable pay component (pay at risk) to replace a portion of fixed compensation costs (annual merit salary increases).
  3. Enhance the strategic planning process.

4. Link incentive award payments to achievement of overall performance objectives.

- Award criteria or formula:

1. Achievement of organizational objectives (50%)—fundraising growth/control of fund-raising costs, net income growth, program service, and delivery goals.
2. Achievement of departmental and individual objectives (50%).

- Award amount:

1. Threshold (meets objectives): 5% of salary-range midpoint
2. Target (exceeds objectives): 10% of salary-range midpoint
3. Maximum (far exceeds objectives): 15% of salary-range midpoint

- Administrative procedures:

1. Review and evaluate achievement of performance objectives at end of year, after financial and other data is available.
2. Senior officers are reviewed and evaluated by the executive director.
3. Executive director is reviewed and evaluated by the compensation committee of the board of directors.
4. All awards are subject to final review and approval by the compensation committee with final approval by the board of directors.

This case study is one example of the use of a Management Incentive Plan. Following is a checklist of design criteria that will help an organization considering such a plan.

Checklist of Design Criteria

The following elements should be considered in evaluating whether to develop a Management Incentive Plan:

- Definition of plan purpose—What are you trying to achieve?

- Determination of how competitive compensation levels of affected staff are relative to the market

- Solicitation of expectations and opinions of key employees—How do affected employees feel about the plan? Do they have a clear understanding of how it works and its potential impact on their compensation level?

- Education of board members on plan purpose and review of their perceptions on the application of such a plan to the organization

- Determination of criteria for plan participation and selection of eligible employees

- Determination of type of plan, award levels, and timing

- Review of strategic plan and establishment of goals and objectives

- Determination of measures of performance (organizational, departmental, individual)

Case Study 2: Discretionary Bonus Plan

Background

This nonprofit agency, with about 200 employees, implemented a discretionary bonus plan approximately four years ago. The purpose of the plan was to recognize extraordinary performance by individuals or by groups of employees *below the senior management level*. The idea to develop such a plan came about as the result of this agency moving to another location. To make the relocation a success, the organization wished to recognize selected staff for their extraordinary efforts over a sustained period of time.

Before developing its discretionary bonus plan guidelines, the nonprofit reviewed several published survey reports on bonus practices. All employees below the senior management level were eligible to participate in the discretionary bonus plan. The following considerations were used by management when determining awards either for an individual or for a group of employees: superior level of performance beyond the scope of regular job duties, substantial cost savings, above-normal overtime hours worked, significant advancement of program objectives or activities.

This nonprofit's review of the competitive survey data for these types of awards indicated an award maximum of 10 percent of salary per year. Accordingly, the organization selected discretionary bonus awards for individuals or groups up to a maximum of 10 percent of salary for a one-year period. Exceptions to the 10 percent maximum were considered for performance of significant additional duties or for projects that exceeded a one-year period, provided no bonus had already been paid. All discretionary bonus recommendations were submitted by the appropriate department heads to human resources for review, with final approval by the executive director.

Summary of Discretionary Bonus Plan Elements

- Eligibility: All employees (individual or group) below the senior management level
- Plan purpose: To recognize extraordinary levels of performance by individuals or groups
- Award criteria or formula: Management discretion, but usually considers the following:
  1. Above-normal overtime hours
  2. Substantial cost savings
  3. Superior performance beyond scope of regular job duties
  4. Significant advancement of program objectives or activities
- Award amount: Bonus award may not exceed 10 percent of salary for a one-year period.

- Administrative procedures:
  1. Administered by the human resources department
  2. All bonus recommendations must be submitted by appropriate department heads to human resources for review; final approval is made by executive director.

This case study is one example of the use of a Discretionary Bonus Plan. Following is a checklist of design criteria that will help an organization considering such a plan.

Checklist of Design Criteria

- Include a broad cross-section of different levels of staff in the design of the program by selecting a staff task team or by using staff focus groups.
- Make sure awards promote and reinforce outstanding performance.
- Develop administrative procedures to ensure equitable administration.
- Communicate the program to all employees, and publicize awards when they are made.
- Give different work units the ability to adapt the program to their own needs.
- Keep the bonus program and base-pay programs separate.
- Continually track, monitor, and evaluate programs to ensure their continued success.

Case Study 3: Spot Award Plan

Background

This large nonprofit organization instituted a spot award program six years ago. *Spot awards* provide immediate recognition in the form of cash for significant staff accomplishments. The organization expected the spot award program to increase staff motivation and loyalty to the organization. Management thought this program would provide an effective tool for establishing a higher standard of performance, as well as for encouraging risk taking and creativity. Also, it was expected that, over time, the quality of work products and the effectiveness of the organization would increase.

The organization wished to promote a better understanding of the overall organization, rather than a focus on one's individual department or work unit. Accordingly, the spot awards were used to recognize team, as well as individual, accomplishments. Management viewed the spot award program as a tool to promote teamwork and cooperation across departments. The expected result included staff development by promoting a sense of ownership in and commitment to the organization.

All employees below the senior management level were eligible to participate in the spot award program. Spot awards were to be awarded only after the fact, that is, at the conclusion of a significant individual or team accomplishment. The criteria for receiving a spot award included the following: significant accomplishments due to effort, time, impact to the organization, and quality of work product; leadership in team or group efforts; display of commitment and accomplishment beyond normal expectations (of an individual or team).

The spot award amounts were to be paid in cash, ranging from $200 to $500, net of taxes. At the discretion of the vice president (department head), the awards could be in $50 increments, based on the level of the accomplishment. The awards were to be paid within thirty days of completion of the exemplary accomplishment. Awards were presented by the executive director at public occasions such as annual meetings and board meetings whenever possible.

All staff members were eligible to make a recommendation of another employee for receipt of an award to a vice president of the recommended employee's department. For team awards affecting employees in several departments, a department vice president nominated and secured the approval of vice presidents in other departments. For team awards, each team member received the same amount when possible. The vice president of finance provides the executive director with a quarterly report on the number of spot awards, recipients, and amounts.

Summary of Spot Award Plan Elements

- Eligibility: All staff below officer level reporting to executive director.
- Plan purposes:
  1. To provide immediate recognition for significant staff or team accomplishments
  2. To encourage risk taking and creativity
  3. To motivate staff to higher performance levels
- Award criteria or formula: For significant accomplishments due to effort, time, impact to the organization, quality of work product, and leadership in team or group efforts
- Award amount: $200 to $500 in cash within thirty days of accomplishment
- Administrative procedures:
  1. All staff members are eligible to make a recommendation of another employee for receipt of an award to a vice president of the recommended employee's department.
  2. For team awards affecting employees in several departments, a department vice president may nominate and secure the approval of vice presidents in other departments.
  3. For team awards, each team member receives the same amount when possible.
  4. The vice president of finance provides the executive director with a quarterly report on the number of spot awards, recipients, and amounts.

5. Awards are presented by the executive director at public occasions such as annual meetings and board meetings whenever possible.

This case study provides an example of one version of a Spot Award Plan. Following is a checklist of design criteria that will help an organization considering such a plan.

Checklist of Design Criteria

Similar to the Discretionary Bonus Plan described in Case Study 2, a Spot Award Program includes many of the same criteria, including:

- Include a broad cross-section of staff in the design of the program.
- Make sure awards promote and reinforce outstanding performance and don't become automatic or "taken for granted."
- Develop administrative procedures to ensure equitable administration.
- Communicate the program to all employees and publicize awards when they are made.
- Continually track, monitor, and evaluate programs to ensure their continued success.

Case Study 4: Noncash Recognition Plan

Background

This is a composite case study, which represents a variety of noncash recognition programs reported in this study. Noncash recognition programs were found in many nonprofit organizations and take a variety of forms. The broad categories of noncash recognition programs included: service awards, suggestion awards, and individual achievement awards.

The purpose of noncash recognition programs is to recognize staff achievements in a tangible way, not including cash, and to thank staff for a job well done. All employees below the managerial levels were eligible, either individually or in teams. The noncash recognition programs were designed to recognize and reward either a specific one-time event or superior performance on a consistent basis. Management discretion was typically used to determine who received a noncash award.

Noncash awards were provided in the following forms: merchandise, plaques, luncheons or dinners, theater or sporting event tickets, choice of gifts, evening out, or savings bonds. The value of the noncash recognition reward was usually under $250. Awards were made within thirty days following the event or the date of notice of such award.

Noncash recognition programs frequently allowed employees to nominate another employee or groups of employees. The human resources department typically monitored and administered noncash recognition programs. For team awards, approval was needed by department heads from each team member's department.

Summary of Noncash Recognition Plan Elements

- Eligibility: All employees, either individual or teams, below the managerial level
- Plan purpose: To recognize staff achievements in a tangible way and to thank staff for a job well done
- Award criteria or formula: Managerial discretion—The program is designed to recognize and reward either a specific unique event or consistent performance beyond expectations.
- Award amount: Includes the following types of awards— merchandise, plaques, luncheons, dinners, theater tickets, evening out. The value is usually under $250. Awards are made within thirty days.
- Administrative procedures:

1. Allows employees to nominate another employee or groups of employees.

2. Human resources department monitors and administers.

3. Approval by department heads for each department.

There are many variations of Noncash Recognition Plans. This case study is one example of the use of a Noncash Recognition Plan. Following is a checklist of design criteria that will help an organization considering such a plan.

Checklist of Design Criteria

- Include a broad cross-section of staff in the design of the program.
- Make sure awards are meaningful and appropriate to the culture of the organization.

Combined with the trend information and the cross-sector study of wage-and-benefit surveys, this section on innovative compensation provides another element to advance your thinking about the approach you should take in your nonprofit organization. Chapter Six will provide action steps for consideration as you begin to apply this knowledge.

REFERENCES

1. National Center for Charitable Statistics, *National Taxonomy of Exempt Entities, Mapping the Nonprofit Sector* (Washington, DC: Independent Sector).

2. James E. Rocco, *Innovative Compensation Practices in the Nonprofit Sector* (Denver, CO: Applied Research and Development Institute International, 1995).

3. James E. Rocco, "Making Incentive Plans Work for Nonprofits," *Nonprofit World* (July/August 1991).

CHAPTER SIX

Moving to Implementation

We have provided, we hope you will agree, a wealth of information on workforce, employment-practice, and compensation trends. It's time now to put this information to work in establishing or augmenting your organization's compensation policies and practices. Brian O'Connell, founding president of Independent Sector, has stated that attracting and retaining able people is an investment in the sector's and your organization's capacity to be of even greater service to people, communities, and causes.

In preparation for this chapter's discussion of establishing and implementing compensation policies, remember that they are part of your human resource management system. Personnel policies, the organization chart, job descriptions, and the performance-appraisal portions of the system are closely related to compensation policies. The Introduction to this book includes an explanation of these relationships. See Exhibit 6.1, The Human Resource Cycle of Activities, and Exhibit 6.2, Human Resources Management System Checklist. Chapter Seven provides referrals to other resources as you continue to develop the compensation and other components of your human resource management system.

Exhibit 6.1   The Human Resource Cycle of Activities

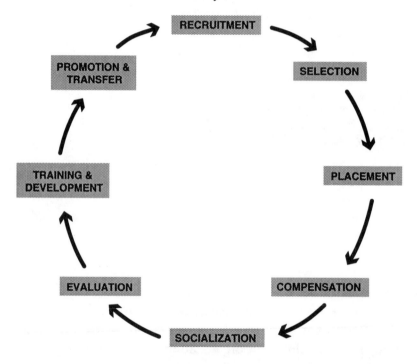

Exhibit 6.2 provides nonprofit organization boards, executives, and managers with a checklist that can assist in determination of developmental work that needs to be undertaken in order to achieve a complete and optimal human resource management system. It covers the major components. Once a component is identified as missing or needing improvement, the leadership of the organization should seek more detailed information on how to develop that area of the system. This book provides referrals to other resources, and ARDI maintains an extensive database of resources and providers of consulting and training assistance.

Exhibit 6.2   Human Resources Management System Checklist

Check each item as to whether you have it in place or not. Then rate those items you have in place by checking the appropriate column. Use your assessment to identify areas that need attention, prioritize those items, and develop an action plan for improvement.

	Have	Don't Have	Fine	Needs Improvement	Un-acceptable
1. Have a written mission statement that clearly and concisely defines the ultimate result that the organization aims to achieve, the general business by which the results are to be achieved, and the beneficiaries that the organization seeks to serve.					
2. Have board members who have the necessary knowledge and experience to lead the board in meeting its responsibilities in regard to human resource management and/or who have obtained such expertise from volunteers or consultants.					
3. Have staff who are capable of working with the board to develop policies and who can implement those policies.					
4. Have a communication plan for ensuring that all employees are aware of the human resource policies and practices of the organization.					
5. Have a human resource philosophy statement that has been adopted by the board of directors.					
6. Have an inventory of all job functions required to conduct the work of the organization.					
7. Have up-to-date job descriptions written for all positions in the organization.					
8. Have an organization chart that clearly shows how the various positions in the organization relate to each other in reporting relationships.					

(continued)

Exhibit 6.2 *(continued)*

	Have	Don't Have	Fine	Needs Improve-ment	Un-accept-able
9. Have written personnel policies that have been reviewed for legal compliance and that are clear and easy to administer and understand.					
10. Have determined the outcomes for our compensation policy.					
11. Have identified the compensation strategies that will lead to achievement of the outcomes for our compensation policy.					
12. Have implemented a compensation plan that is internally equitable and externally competitive.					
13. Have an evaluation mechanism in place that will provide feedback on how well the strategies are achieving the outcomes sought.					
14. Have an affirmative action policy, which at least meets legal requirements, and have ensured that the policy is followed in all related employment practices.					
15. Are aware of all legal compliance and reporting requirements related to human resource management and are in adherence.					
16. Have developed employee orientation and training appropriate to all employees.					
17. Have personnel records that are complete and appropriate.					
18. Have a performance-appraisal system that provides constructive feedback to employees and that provides appropriate motivation for improved performance.					
19. Have a process for annual review of human resource policy to determine if any adjustments need to be made.					

ROLES AND RELATIONSHIPS

Ultimately, the board of directors has the final responsibility for ensuring that the organization has established compensation policies and is consistently implementing them. The "intermediate sanctions" provisions signed into law in July 1996 spell out board responsibility (see Appendix C for articles on the intermediate sanctions). The goal of this law is to ensure that the directors satisfy duty-of-care standards to ensure that the organization's resources are used prudently and carefully. The Internal Revenue Service and state law require a nonprofit corporation to be "reasonable" in compensation and not to provide the equivalents of economic benefits. It is important to have a process for determining compensation that is thoughtful and deliberate. A nonprofit must show independence of the decision makers on the board from those receiving compensation. Further, the board must demonstrate appropriate reliance on data regarding comparability of compensation. Finally, the decisions and actions on compensation should be adequately documented. (1, 9, 13)

The board has direct responsibility for the employment and the establishment of the compensation of the top executive of the nonprofit corporation. (5) The board also has direct responsibility for establishing the overall compensation policies and for oversight of the implementation of the policies. It then delegates administration of the compensation policies it establishes to the executive, who must ensure that all supervisors in the organization understand and comply with these policies as they administer the compensation for individuals whom they supervise.

The executive should work with the board to determine what oversight information it should review and at what intervals in order to monitor policy compliance. The executive also provides information and staff support to the board in policy development.

In practice, a large board may wish to establish a three-to-five-member compensation committee or to create a subsidiary unit within a committee focusing on administration or human resources. The responsibility of this committee or unit is to conduct studies and prepare reports and recommendations for review and action by the full board. A smaller board may need to work as a committee of the whole.

Whatever the work group used, the relevant expertise should be sought—law, accounting, finance, nonprofit management, and human resource management. This expertise can be from directors or other volunteers who are recruited to assist. Members of the compensation committee should have no financial or significant social or personal relationship with the chief executive or other staff. Employees can supply expert information and do the leg work, but they should not be directly involved in decision making because they have an inherent conflict of interest. Consultants can be very valuable to boards in adding expertise. (6) See Exhibit 6.5 on page 132, A Checklist for Development of a Compensation Policy, to assess or guide your organization's process.

STEPS IN ESTABLISHING A COMPENSATION POLICY

A nonprofit organization defines its success by how well it performs in accomplishing its mission. Compensation policy can be an important tool to maximize employee contributions toward goal achievement and mission success, and it should be vested within the mission and goals of the organization. Other factors to be aware of when beginning to set compensation policies are the values and culture within the organization and environmental and market demands.

Taking these overarching factors into account, the first step the compensation committee should take is to determine what the organization wants to accomplish with its compensation policy. Edward Lawler (7) noted the need to identify the outcomes needed from the compensation. Two examples of desired outcomes, among many, are retention of specialized, highly skilled employees with high desirability to other employers and increased productivity of existing employees. Exhibit 6.3 is an example of a human resources philosophy statement.

Exhibit 6.3   Example of a Human Resources Philosophy Statement

Applied Research and Development Institute International, Inc.

Human Resource Philosophy Statement

The mission of the Applied Research and Development Institute International, Inc. (ARDI) is to strengthen the management and leadership of public benefit non-profit organizations so they will have increased capacity to improve their communities and society.

ARDI accomplishes this mission through advocating the importance of effective management and leadership; broadening access to resources; integrating related knowledge from the governmental, for-profit, and nonprofit sectors; and developing and testing new management approaches.

To accomplish this mission:

- ARDI will put the well-being of society and the nonprofit sector and its ability to serve the public good above its own needs.
- ARDI will employ and promote collaborative, inclusive, and collegial processes.
- ARDI will actively seek to avoid duplication and waste of efforts so that the resources of the nonprofit sector are used to greater impact.
- ARDI will employ the highest standards of management and leadership in its own organization.

As part of the strategy, our personnel policies, practices, and programs must:

- Attract qualified employees.
- Seek out highly motivated individuals who demonstrate an exceptional potential for success.
- Encourage the mentality of "self-starters" and individual responsibility.
- Design a compensation program that reflects internal equity and the external market.
- Promote efficient management of our resources.
- Remain flexible yet consistent by maintaining stability in senior management and administrative personnel.
- Offer intern opportunities that add value and support the operations of ARDI and at the same time meet the learning goals of the interns.
- Acknowledge that project-specific personnel may experience turnover based on funding.

Recruiting and Career Development

- We believe in hiring the most qualified people available and, whenever possible and appropriate, promote from within the ARDI staff. For each position, we will identify the required characteristics and fill the position with a person possessing the necessary skills.
- We attempt to recruit people who are team-oriented and who demonstrate leadership qualities.

(continued)

Exhibit 6.3 *(continued)*

- We provide a supportive environment that encourages employees to take advantage of opportunities for personal and professional development.

Compensation

- We believe in a total compensation program that is market-based and that helps us attract and retain a high quality workforce.
- We believe our compensation program should reward those employees who contribute to our commitment to excellence.
- We believe the compensation level for each job should be established through an objective analysis.

Benefits

- We believe benefits are an important component of our total compensation package.

Performance Management and Training

- We believe there must be a consistent performance-management process throughout ARDI, however the performance measures may vary, based on the level or nature of the job.
- The performance-management process should include ongoing discussions between employees and supervisors and should include both informal and formal evaluation processes.
- We believe both results and efforts toward achieving results are important and that results should be measured against job standards and performance goals.

Communications

- We believe in the importance of open, honest, respectful, and regular communication among all members of our organization.
- We believe communication includes listening as well as talking. We expect and encourage our employees to express their opinions and to offer suggestions to improve ARDI and increase our impact.

Human Resource Program Administration

- We strive for simplicity in design and administration.
- We believe in providing general policy guidelines to ensure human resource programs are consistently applied, but we also believe in giving management sufficient flexibility to deal with special situations.
- We do not discriminate in employment practice, career growth, or other opportunities on the basis of race, sex, sexual preference, ethnicity, religion, national origin, marital status, age, disability, or veteran status.

As the compensation committee begins its work to identify outcomes, it can start by obtaining initial input on recruitment, motivation, retention, and any other compensation concerns from the board of directors, the executive, and other managers. From this input, the committee can formulate a draft outcome statement for the compensation program. It may wish to circulate the statement to the board, the executive, and the other managers for reaction before finalizing it. Those outcomes become the measure against which the success of the policy will be evaluated.

The next step is to conduct a review of the present situation in regard to the job descriptions and their relationship to one another. The relative value of various jobs to the organization should be reviewed. It is important that the job descriptions and the organization chart be up-to-date prior to gathering information on market pricing. The executive is usually responsible for preparing this information for review by the committee. In situations where the board feels the need for a zero-based review, a consultant may be retained to conduct such a study. See Exhibit 6.4, Sample Job Description Format.

Exhibit 6.4   Sample Job-Description Format

NAME OF ORGANIZATION

MISSION STATEMENT

POSITION TITLE

POSITION SUMMARY

POSITION ACCOUNTABILITIES

(continued)

Exhibit 6.4 *(continued)*

JOB SPECIFICATIONS

- Minimum Education
- Preferred Education
- Required Experience
- Preferred Experience
- Required Skills
- Preferred Skills
- Physical Demands

SUPERVISION EXERCISED

SUPERVISION RECEIVED

The above statements are intended to describe the general nature and level of work being performed. They are not intended to be construed as an exhaustive list of all responsibilities, duties, and skills required of personnel so classified.

EEO/M/F

There are now many sources of information specific to compensation in nonprofit organizations that can aid the committee. Some of them have been used in the cross-sector and innovative compensation study, and Chapter Seven provides additional referral information. Note that some positions are nonprofit specific, such as development director, and, therefore, the nonprofit wage-and-benefit data will be all that is required. Other positions are recruited across sectors, for example, secretary, and market pricing will need to meet the general community standard. An article in *Personnel Journal*, June 1995, entitled "Look before You Leap," (6) cautions that you should consider the following compensation-survey variables and check for comparability to your organization before assigning too much weight to the survey data:

- Size of organizations surveyed in both budget size and number of employees

- Industries included
- Type of organization
- Geographic region served

We would add to this list the geographic location of your organization compared to the survey data as an important variable.

A comparison can now be made between the compensation that your organization offers by position and the survey data. The comparison should be a check both on internal equity and for position relative to external competition. You may find that a job title or actual set of responsibilities cannot be directly compared. This is where benchmarking comes into use. Earlier you determined the relationship of the positions in your organization to one another and their relative value to your organization. You can now align surveyed benchmark positions to positions particular to your organization, slotting them into the compensation scale according to higher job requirements or lower job requirements. This will provide guidance about compensation levels and their relative relationships even when direct survey data is not available.

As the compensation committee progresses in its work, it should consider innovative compensation plans. We noted earlier in the book that use of innovative compensation plans has grown over the past several years in response to new working arrangements and expectations of both employees and employers. According to Gross and McCullough from The Hay Group, variable pay programs have been used for many years and continue to be used in for-profit organizations for the following reasons (15):

- To support a participative culture
- To reinforce total quality management processes
- To align employees' pay with business results

- To suppress entitlement mentality
- To encourage employee stakeholdership
- To communicate values to employees
- To focus employees' activities

Crystal and Silberman (2) cite that for-profits pursue such plans to obtain the following results:

- To lower the ratio of fixed costs to variable costs, thereby giving the organization greater ability to withstand economic downturns
- To reward superior performance without simultaneously rewarding poor performance
- To signal managers about what the organization considers important objectives

The compensation committee will want to determine if any of those results are among the outcomes they have identified for their compensation plan. If so, they should at least consider some of the innovative plans discussed in Chapter Five to see if they should be utilized as part of their overall package.

Exhibit 6.5   A Checklist for Development of a Compensation Policy

Exhibit 6.5 provides a checklist of critical action steps to follow as you undertake to update or formulate compensation policies for your nonprofit organization.

I.   **Recruiting a Compensation Committee**

   A.   A *work unit* of the board of directors will be responsible for the development of the compensation policies. The work unit can be a committee, a subcommittee, or in the case of a small board, the board itself. The size of the work unit can vary depending upon the structure of the organization (typical work units or committees range from three to five members). For the remainder of this checklist, "work unit" will be referred to as the "compensation committee."

B. The board should develop and authorize, according to the bylaws or traditional means, a written compensation committee charge, including responsibilities and procedures.

C. The members of the compensation committee should have the necessary knowledge to accomplish the work. Examples of professionals with relevant knowledge are attorney, accountant, human resource specialist, and nonprofit management specialist.

D. Members of the committee should not have financial or other significant social or personal relationships with the executive or other staff. The executive should ensure that the committee has adequate support, but the executive is not a member of the committee. Compensation committee members may need to be recruited from outside of the board according to the need for additional expertise.

    Your potential compensation committee candidates have been identified and the recruitment process begun. List potential candidates below:

    _____   _____

    _____   _____

    _____   _____

    _____   _____

    Recruitment of the compensation committee has been completed according to the criteria in C and D above. The final roster includes the following members:

    _____   _____

    _____   _____

    _____   _____

    A chair with strong leadership skills has been appointed.

    _____

    These next steps are to be completed by the compensation committee with the support of the organization's executive and staff members. The organization's board of directors is responsible for final approval of the policies.

    (continued)

	Yes	No

II. Preparation for Developing Your Organization's Compensation Policies

A. Gather Internal Background Information

    1. Material has been assembled to inform the compensation committee about the current status of the organization. The material should include:

        • Mission statement

        • Current job descriptions

        • Vision statement

        • No. of people in each position

        • Values

        • Organization chart

        • Relevant organization history

        • Personnel policies

        • Organizational culture

        • Summarized employee info. (demographics, tenure, etc.)

    2. Information on your organization's current compensation policies and practices has been obtained (including wage scales, benefits, and innovative compensation practices).

    3. Input has been solicited from the board, executive, and managers and supervisors regarding workforce concerns related to compensation policies.

    4. Current employee motivations and those of prospective employee markets have been identified.

B. Gather External Background Information

    1. Appropriate workforce and market-pricing data has been obtained and reviewed and any additional data generated as needed.

    2. Innovative compensation practices have been reviewed to determine which ones are of interest.

	Yes	No
C. Identify Desired Outcomes		
1. Outcomes to be achieved from the compensation policies have been identified and agreed to by the organization leadership.		
2. Determination has been made as to the adequacy of data, and additional data has been gathered as needed.		
3. The need for a consultant has been determined and obtained as necessary.		
III. Update/Alter Current Policies and Practices to Reflect Desired Outcomes		
A. The organization chart, job descriptions, and related sections of the personnel policies have been reviewed and are revised as needed to meet current conditions.		
B. Basic wage scales and benefits have been revised or established.		
C. Equity in current compensation within the organization has been reviewed, and any corrective actions have been identified and addressed.		
D. Employee reactions to prospective innovative practices have been obtained.		
E. Additional advice or information has been obtained to allow for choices to be made about which, if any, innovative practices fit the organization's need.		
F. Decisions have been made on the innovative compensation practices that will be included/incorporated into current or new compensation policies.		
IV. Implement New Policies		
A. An integrated compensation plan has been developed.		
B. The board has approved the plan, and monitoring and evaluation mechanisms are in place.		
C. The plan has been communicated to employees.		

SPECIAL CONSIDERATIONS

The compensation mix must be considered in relation to organization resources; market price data; the values and culture of the organization; workforce, compensation, and employment-practice trends; and the preferences of both prospective and current employees. We have provided information in this book on traditional wages and benefits, plus various cash, recognition, and innovative benefit programs. Before delving further into the steps in establishing your organization's compensation plan, let's consider some information regarding work-related motivations of certain subcategories of the workforce from which you may be recruiting.

Women comprise 68 percent of the nonprofit workforce. The high percentage is the result of a variety of factors, including but not limited to women's traditional involvement in and desire to work toward improving society and higher barriers facing women in entering and advancing in the historically white-male-dominated business sector. As businesses begin to look beyond the traditional white male population, women will be more in demand. Adequate salaries and benefits are certainly an issue for many women. Other factors nonprofits should consider to recruit and retain women are job-sharing, part-time jobs, flexible hours and days, child care, and sick leave for family illness. The content of the work is also important to women (3, 7, 11).

Young people seeking first employment are among the shrinking segments of the workforce. Competition for these young workers will be great; however, the nonprofit work environment is well matched to their motivations. Because nonprofits often have a small number of employees and fewer specialists, they can offer young workers immediate access to the important work of the organization and rapid skill development. On the negative side, nonprofits often don't have rapid promotion opportunities, so retention is more of a challenge. Salaries and benefits may often be a critical factor after early skill-development rewards are exhausted.

Second careerists are a newer resource for nonprofits. As business and government reduce middle management and offer early retirement packages, a population is growing that may prove very helpful to nonprofits. Drucker (4) and Lee (12) state that such workers are prepared to take pay cuts, but not of the size indicated by the data in the current study. This group of older workers is concerned with health benefits, job security, and pensions. Nonprofits who wish to recruit from this workforce segment may need to close the compensation gap some and examine their pension offerings. Generous policies regarding nonconflicting outside employment may be another way of improving overall compensation. For retirees, job-sharing, flexibility in hours, days, times of year, and method of accomplishing the job are all important (17, 5).

Crossover employees, especially those from the for-profit sector, may need cultural and other special training to help them adapt to and be productive in the nonprofit environment. It seems worth the effort because this segment of the population is growing. Crossover employees may be in a financial position where their accumulated assets, and/or carryover benefits, enable them to accept lower salaries and benefits in the nonprofit sector.

Nonprofit organizations often operate their service programs in a culturally diverse atmosphere, and as a result, they often extensively employ *minority workers*. Many believe the nonprofit sector should, or does, hold a strong value system regarding cultural diversity. Because of this, the sector may be in a good position to successfully recruit and retain minority and immigrant workers. It should go without saying, but we will say it anyway, *equal pay for equal work regardless of gender, race, ethnicity, religion, sexual orientation, or age* is a moral, ethical, and sometimes legal imperative for nonprofit organizations. The legal guidelines outlined in the Equal Employment Opportunities Law can be found in Exhibit 6.6.

Resources are often very tight and nonprofits cannot as readily pass along increased personnel costs to customers and clients as businesses can, nor can they pass tax increases or increase debt as government can. Therefore, in addition to paying employees an adequate wage and at least minimum benefits (such as vacation, sick leave, and health, life, and disability insurance), nonprofits need to be aware of the emotional and social benefits they can offer. They will also need to be creative in deployment of these methods of compensation. Nonprofits can offer considerable worker satisfaction by making a match between work and employee interests and by providing employees with a sense that they are making a positive difference through their work.

There are many other low-cost tools that nonprofits can use to improve the ability to recruit and retain quality employees. Some low-cost actions a nonprofit can take to improve its compensation and employment practices are:

- Support participation in relevant training programs for staff
- Utilize existing benefit pools, create benefit pools through coalitions, or lease employees to enrich benefits or to control costs
- Enhance noncash benefits, such as leave time
- Create generous policies regarding outside employment, in addition to the position held in the nonprofit organization, while controlling for conflict-of-interest situations
- Create a flexible workplace environment, including consideration of work at home
- Institute recognition programs, including written, verbal, private, and public acknowledgments of employees
- Join in creative barter or special discount arrangements with other nonprofits that offer services of interest to their employees

Attention to building an overall and quality human-resource-management system increases job satisfaction. Having members of the board with expertise in human resource development provides in-house leadership for this effort. The executive and other managers may need to have access to training programs or to consultants to help them develop this function.

Exhibit 6.6   Equal Employment Opportunity is the Law

PRIVATE EMPLOYMENT, STATE AND LOCAL GOVERNMENTS, EDUCATIONAL INSTITUTIONS

RACE, COLOR, RELIGION, SEX, NATIONAL ORIGIN:

Title VII of the Civil Rights Act of 1964 as amended, prohibits discrimination in hiring, promotion, discharge, pay, fringe benefits, and other aspects of employment on the basis of race, color, religion, sex or national origin.

The law covers applicants to and employees of most private employers, state and local governments and public or private educational institutions. Employment agencies, labor unions and apprenticeship programs also are covered.

AGE:

The Age Discrimination in Employment Act of 1967, as amended, prohibits age discrimination and protects applicants and employees 40 years of age or older from discrimination on account of age in hiring, promotion, discharge, compensation, terms, conditions, or privileges of employment. The law covers applicants to and employees of most private employers, state and local governments, educational institutions, employment agencies and labor organizations.

SEX (WAGES):

In addition to sex discrimination prohibited by Title VII of the Civil Rights Act (see above), the Equal Pay Act of 1963, as amended, prohibits sex discrimination in payment of wages to women and men performing substantially equal work in the same establishment. The law covers applicants to and employees of most private employers, state and local governments and most educational institutions. Labor organizations cannot cause employers to violate the law. Many employers not covered by Title VII, because of size, are covered by the equal pay act.

DISABILITY:

The Americans with Disabilities Act of 1990, as amended, prohibits discrimination on the basis of disability, and protects qualified applicants and employees with disabilities from discrimination in hiring, promotion, discharge, pay, job training, fringe benefits, and other aspects of employment. The law also requires that covered entities provide qualified applicants and employees with disabilities with reasonable accommodations that do not impose undue hardship. The law covers applicants to and employees of most private employers, state and local governments, educational institutions, employment agencies and labor organizations.

If you believe that you have been discriminated against under any of the above laws, you immediately should contact:

The U.S. Equal Employment Opportunity Commission [EEOC], 1301 L Street, N.W., Washington, DC 20507.

FEDERAL HOLDING FEDERAL CONTRACTS OR SUBCONTRACTS

RACE, COLOR, RELIGION, SEX, NATIONAL ORIGIN:

Executive Order 11246, as amended, prohibits job discrimination on the basis

(continued)

of race, color, religion, sex, or national origin, and requires affirmative action to ensure equality of opportunity in all aspects of employment.

INDIVIDUALS WITH HANDICAPS:

Section 503 of the Rehabilitation Act of 1973, as amended, prohibits job discrimination because of handicap and requires affirmative action to employ and advance in employment qualified individuals with handicaps who, with reasonable accommodation, can perform the essential functions of a job.

VIETNAM ERA AND SPECIAL DISABLED VETERANS:

38 U.S.C. 4212 of the Vietnam Era Veterans Readjustment Assistance Act of 1974 prohibits job discrimination and requires affirmative action to employ and advance in employment qualified Vietnam era veterans and qualified special disabled veterans.

Applicants to and employees of companies with a Federal government contract or subcontract are protected under the authorities above. Any person who believes a contractor has violated its nondiscrimination or affirmative action obligations under Executive Order 11246, as amended, Section 503 of the Rehabilitation Act or 38 U.S.C. 4212 of the Vietnam Era Veterans Readjustment Assistance Act should contact immediately:

The Office of Federal Contract Compliance Programs [OFCCP] Employment Standards Administration, U.S. Department of Labor: 200 Constitution Avenue, N.W., Washington, DC 20210, or an OFCCP regional or district office, listed in most telephone directories under U.S. Government, Department of Labor.

PROGRAMS OR ACTIVITIES RECEIVING FEDERAL FINANCIAL ASSISTANCE

RACE, COLOR, NATIONAL ORIGIN, SEX:

In addition to the protection of Title VII of the Civil Rights Act 1964, Title VI of the Civil Rights Act prohibits discrimination on the basis of race, color or national origin in programs or activities receiving Federal financial assistance. Employment discrimination covered by Title VI if the primary objective of the financial assistance is provision of employment or where employment discrimination causes or may cause discrimination in providing services under such programs. Title IX of the Education Amendments of 1972 prohibits employment discrimination on the basis of sex in educational programs or activities which receive Federal assistance.

If you believe you have been discriminated against in a program by any institution which receives Federal assistance, you should contact immediately the Federal agency providing such assistance.

INDIVIDUALS WITH HANDICAPS:

Section 504 of the Rehabilitation Act of 1973, as amended, prohibits employment discrimination on the basis of handicap in a program or activity which receives Federal financial assistance. Discrimination is prohibited in all aspects of employment against handicapped persons who, with reasonable accommodation, can perform the essential functions of a job.

FORMULATING THE COMPENSATION PLAN

It's decision time. The committee has accumulated a great deal of information about current employees, recruitment and retention issues, status of jobs, compensation, and employment conditions. They have identified the outcomes they are to achieve with the compensation plan. They have obtained market-price comparisons for all positions for which they are establishing compensation and they have examined the information regarding innovative strategies. The committee should then take the following steps:

1.   Decide on the mix of compensation types and employment-practice strategies they wish to use. It is now possible to establish or to update the wage scales for each job and to establish the benefits that the organization will offer all employees. One decision is in regards to where in the market range the organization wishes to place its pay. For example, you can employ at the top of the competitive pay range and recruit the most able and experienced workers in the market or you can employ at an average or middle range, knowing that you may need to invest in longer, more extensive on-the-job training to grow employee capabilities. You may select different market pricing for different positions. Each position will have a minimum, medium, and maximum wage identified. This range from minimum to maximum is usually between 30 percent and 50 percent, (6) with larger ranges for positions higher in the organization's job and related-wage structure. The larger ranges for positions requiring higher skill levels and greater responsibilities reflect the need to retain such employees over a longer period of time.

2.   Determine who is eligible to participate in the various innovative strategies that are chosen because innovative practices such as incentive pay may not be relevant for all positions. The same is true for employment practices such as flextime or work at home. Some practices may be appropriate for some positions

but not for others. However, base pay and benefits are relevant for all positions. Achieving a fair and competitive level through these traditional reward systems should be component #1 of the compensation package. The caveat to this is that the committee must have in mind how much emphasis they are placing on base pay and benefits versus compensation of an innovative nature prior to finalizing the base-pay and benefit recommendations.

3. Establish fair and competitive base-compensation levels for all positions if your nonprofit has not instituted innovative strategies previously and wishes to take an interim step. This step will place you in a known position in relation to market pricing. You may also be able to select some easy-to-implement, noncontroversial, and low-cost adjuncts to your basic pay and benefit plan. An example might be to establish an employee recognition program or to implement flextime. You can then commission a study, with or without consulting assistance, of the innovative programs in which you are most interested.

4. Obtain an expert review of the proposed compensation plan to ensure it is in compliance with relevant laws. An expert in compensation or an attorney practicing in this field should be able to provide such a review. Having received and acted upon expert advice, the committee is now ready to present their recommendations to the board for review/revision or adoption.

Once this is done, the appropriate board leadership and the executive should ensure all staff members are informed of any changes in the compensation plan for the organization and why they were made. In Chapter 24 of Robert Herman's *Handbook of Leadership and Management* (8), Nancy E. Day cites that, at minimum, employees should be told:

- The methods by which jobs were analyzed
- The policy in regard to reactions to market rates

- How performance relates to pay
- How pay increases are determined and administered
- Government and economic limits on compensation levels
- Administration policies and procedures

A feedback loop should be instituted for any new compensation strategies so that after a reasonable period of time, their impact on the desired outcome can be ascertained and any corrections or additions made (8).

The board should plan for its compensation committee to review and possibly adjust jobs and the compensation program annually; however, an extensive planning exercise such as described previously need not be done each year. Complete reexamination of the compensation plan might be appropriate at three-year intervals or when some other special condition arises, for example, during a merger or to a move to a new region of the country or when significant changes in the workforce market occur, such as the recent resetting of the minimum wage. It would be wise to subscribe to a publication that summarizes case law and other laws regarding administration of compensation and/ or to establish a relationship with an attorney and/or human resource specialist who could identify how changes in laws and regulations may affect your organization.

For some of you with considerable previous knowledge and experience with compensation management in nonprofits, this book provides an opportunity to review, reflect, and update your information. For others, this may be a beginning step to gain mastery over this function for which you have or will have considerable responsibility. In the second situation, consider Chapter Seven and the Bibliography as a guide to further learning. In either case, we urge you to take action within your nonprofit to ensure that you have established compensation programs that will enable you to recruit and retain your most important asset, the staff for your organization.

REFERENCES

1. Bondi & Co. LLP, "New Legislation—What You Need to Know for Your Organization," *Nonprofit Agendas: Managing a Nonprofit in a For-Profit World* (February/March 1997).

2. Graef S. Crystal and Samuel J. Silberman, "Not-for-Profit Organizations Need Incentive Compensation," *Personnel Journal* (April 1986).

3. Claudia A. Deutsch, "It's Job, Not Benefits for Women Executives," *Denver Post* (25 June 1990).

4. Peter Drucker, "Peter Drucker on the Non-profit Environment," *The Taft Non-profit Executive* 9, no. 3 (November 1989).

5. Diedre Fanning, "Retirement: Does it Kill Executives?," *New York Times* (29 May 1990).

6. Gillian Flynn, "Look before you leap: Not all salary surveys are created equal," *Personnel Journal* 74 (June 1995).

7. Ellen Goldschmidt, "Careers with a Conscience," *Self* (September 1989).

8. Robert D. Herman, *The Jossey-Bass Handbook of Nonprofit Leadership and Management* (San Francisco: Jossey-Bass Publishers, 1994).

9. Daniel L. Kurtz, "Fixing Nonprofit Executive Compensation," *VCG boardmember's FORUM* (New York: Volunteer Consulting Group, 1996).

10. Edward E. Lawler III, *Pay for Performance: A Motivational Analysis*, School of Business Administration, University of Southern California.

11. Julia Lawler, "Cracks in the Glass Ceiling," *USA Today* (June 1990).

12. Tony Lee, "Non-profits Ready to Compete for Corporate Executives," *National Business Employment Weekly* (December 1988).

13. John Murawski, "Law Penalizing Lavish Nonprofit Salaries Causes Uncertainty," *Chronicle of Philanthropy* 8, no. 23 (19 September 1996).

14. National Center for Nonprofit Boards, "The Nonprofit Board's Guide to Chief Executive Compensation," *Board Member* 4, no. 5 (August 1995).

15. New York Compensation Association, "Alternative Rewards: Do

They Work?" *Workforce Compensation* (New York: New York Compensation Association, 1993).

16. Brian O'Connell, "Salaries in Nonprofit Organizations," *Nonprofit World* 10 (July/August 1991).

17. Taft Group, "The Greying American Workforce," *The Taft Non-profit Executive* 9, no. 7 (February 1990).

CHAPTER SEVEN

Where to Go for Further Help

As discussed in Chapter 6, developing your organization's compensation policies can be a difficult and complicated task. Yet, the process can be made easier if you begin by accessing resources (books, manuals, videos, surveys, etc.) that:

- Provide guidelines on developing compensation policies and model policies used by similar organizations
- Include wage-and-benefit data
- Deal with information on related personnel issues, such as personnel policy and job-description development

Interviewing colleagues and other contacts from similar organizations in your area can also provide you with some ideas about how to structure your compensation policies. Finally, access to expert advice and consultation (in many cases legal advice) is often necessary, and ARDI recommends that you submit your final compensation plan to an attorney for review.

This chapter will provide you with a sampling of resources, in addition to the chapter references and bibliography, and contacts to connect you to additional assistance as you update or develop compensation policies for your organization. ARDI encourages readers to contact the individuals and organizations listed here to obtain more information about each resource or service prior to purchasing them for your organization (ARDI has not reviewed all of the resources and provides information on them only as a point of reference).

RESOURCES THAT INCLUDE GUIDELINES AND SAMPLE COMPENSATION POLICIES

The 1996 "Management and Leadership Resources for Nonprofits" directory, compiled by ARDI, includes a reference section on Human Resource Management (HRM) that includes descriptions and ordering information for 219 resources (books, manuals, tapes, etc.). Many of these resources include information on setting up compensation policies as well as wage-and-benefit data sources from across the country. More information on this directory can be obtained through ARDI at (303) 691-6076. The directory will be available on-line in the spring of 1998 at http:/www.ardi.org.

The Nonprofit Management Handbook: Operating Policies and Procedures. This 1993 publication, written by Tracy Daniel Connors, includes information, sample forms, and examples to help nonprofits create their own policy manuals and to manage and administer their organizations—available through John Wiley & Sons, Inc., (800) 753-0655.

Executive Compensation: A Primer for Board Members and Chief Executives. This overview of executive compensation includes a review of the factors that affect the level of compensation, a checklist for determining compensation, and a discussion of the responsibilities of board members in the process—available through the National Center for Nonprofit Boards, (202) 452-6262.

The Jossey-Bass Handbook of Nonprofit Leadership and Management. Edited by Robert D. Herman in 1994, this book consists of articles by nonprofit-sector researchers on managing nonprofit organizations, including a chapter on designing and managing compensation and benefit programs. The handbook also includes a section that describes the Point-Factor Evaluation. This common job-evaluation method includes identifying and weighing a set of factors that describe job characteristics, establishing levels within each factor and assigning points to the levels, and then comparing the jobs to these factors. The resulting point totals for each job allow an organization to structure their pay scales and evaluation procedures accordingly—available through Jossey-Bass, (415) 433-1767.

Compensation in Not-for-Profit Organizations. This publication includes survey data on nonprofit wages and benefits, as well as information on establishing and implementing compensation policies. The book also includes information on innovative practices that nonprofits are using—available through Coopers & Lybrand, (212) 259-3095.

WAGE-AND-BENEFIT SURVEYS

The information and data found in wage-and-benefit surveys can provide you with a profile of the various options and levels of compensation used by other nonprofit organizations. Following are descriptions of the surveys that ARDI used in developing the data analysis for the wage-and-benefit study in Chapter Six. Some are national in scope; however, when developing your own compensation practices, regional or local comparisons may also be useful. If none of the surveys in this section are representative of your area, ARDI recommends that you contact a local nonprofit management support organization or your state association of nonprofits in order to find relevant data.

• "1995 Nonprofit Salary and Benefits Survey of the Greater Kansas City Area." Published by the Center for Management Assistance, this survey includes salary information on thirty-eight positions by budget size, gender, and organization type. The survey also includes a benefits section that focuses on trends, leave time, sick leave, insurance, retirement, and other benefits— available through the Center for Management Assistance, (816) 283-3000.

• "1995 Survey of New York Metropolitan Area Not-for-Profit Organizations, Compensation and Benefits." Published by Ernst & Young LLP, this survey presents salary data from 212 organizations by budget size, type of organization, and number of employees. Eighteen positions commonly found in nonprofit organizations are included. Some benefit information is also provided on medical plan increases, vacation and holiday plans, retirement, insurance disability, and tuition reimbursement— available through Ernst & Young LLP, Not-for-Profit Business Services, (212) 773-3000.

• "1996 Management Compensation Report, Not-for-Profit Organizations." Published by Towers Perrin, this survey provides a range of data on fifty-six positions, including total cash compensation and base salaries by location, organization type, budget, total employees, and time in position. This survey also analyzes management practices, five-year trends, and benefits (pensions and other retirement plans, medical, and variable compensation practices)—available through Towers Perrin, (703) 351-4700.

• "1996 Wage & Benefit Survey of Northern California Nonprofit Organizations." Published by the Management Center, this survey includes data from 345 organizations in Northern California. The data is organized by job function (program services, administration, arts, and office) and position (e.g., "Office: Typing/Filing)." The level of responsibility within each position further divides the data. Salary data includes budget size, gender, education of employee, experience, location, and field of service. Salary median, average, and the 25th and 75th percentiles are noted. Benefit information includes time off, insurance, retirement, and policy and procedures—available through the Management Center, (415) 362-9735.

• "Compensation in Nonprofit Organizations, 9th Edition." This survey, published by Abbott, Langer & Associates, includes salary data on over 100 positions provided by 1,761 organizations. The positions are organized by job function (e.g., clerical or fiscal). Each job position includes salary data analyzed by all respondents, level of supervision, type of organization, number of employees, annual budget, scope of the organization (international, national, regional, state, local), and location. The survey provides mean, first decile, first quartile, median, third quartile, and ninth decile salary figures—available through Abbott, Langer & Associates, (708) 672-4200.

• "Compensation of Chief Executive Officers in Nonprofit Organizations, 9th Edition." Published by Abbott, Langer & Associates, this survey is organized like the "Compensation in Nonprofit Organizations, 9th Edition" and focuses exclusively on the salaries of chief executive officers (CEOs)—available through Abbott, Langer & Associates, (708) 672-4200.

• "Delaware Nonprofit Wage & Benefit Survey, 1996 Edition." Published by the Delaware Association of Nonprofit Agencies, this publication includes survey data from 103 organizations reporting on 117 positions. Salary data is presented by budget size and includes range, mean, and average. Benefit data is presented for insurance, eligibility, holidays, vacation, sick leave, and other perquisites. Additional information on employment policies is also included—available through the Delaware Association of Nonprofit Agencies, (302) 777-5500.

• "Salaries and Benefits in Youth Development Agencies." Published by the National Collaboration for Youth, National Assembly of National Voluntary Health and Social Welfare Organizations, this survey is based on information provided by 1,050 community-based organizations from across the United States. Salary data is presented on fifty-eight positions and is organized by budget size, number of employees, and region. Benefit data for full- and part-time employees is provided, including health care, vacation, sick time, flexible benefits, salary increases, retirement, supplemental benefits for CEOs, and severance pay—available through the National Assembly, (202) 347-2080.

In addition to the surveys that ARDI analyzed in its wage-and-benefit study, there are a number of recent surveys available that may be in a geographic region or have a service type closer to your own organization:

- "1996 Wage and Benefit Survey for Nonprofit Organizations in Southern California," available from the Center for Nonprofit Management in Southern California, (213) 623-7080.

- "Association Executive Compensation Study, 9th Edition," available from the American Society of Association Executives (202) 626-2748.

- "Christian Ministries Salary Survey, 14th Edition," available from the Christian Management Association, (800) 727-4262.

- "Foundation Salary Report," available from the Council on Foundations, (202) 467-0427.

- "Colorado Springs Nonprofit Center Salary and Benefits Survey 1995," available from the Chamber Foundation, P.O. Box B, Colorado Springs, CO 80901.

- "Not-for-Profit Salary Report, 1994–1995," available from the United Way of Greater St. Louis, (314) 421-0700.

- "Tennessee Nonprofit Salary and Benefit Survey," available from the Council of Community Services, (615) 385-2221.

- "Wage and Benefit Survey—Texas Gulf Coast Area," available from the Management Assistance Program/United Way of the Texas Gulf Coast, (718) 685-1963.

RESOURCES THAT PROVIDE INFORMATION ON RELATED PERSONNEL ISSUES

Compensation is only one component of an integrated Human Resource Management plan. Nonprofit organizations should make sure that, in addition to a well-thought-out set of compensation practices, they have a clear set of personnel policies, a consistent and well-documented hiring process, and an organized administrative system that can handle all of these components. Again, ARDI recommends consulting with an expert while developing these components. The following resources may be helpful in developing an integrated human resource plan:

Employment and Personnel: A Legal Handbook. Edited by Richard S. Hobish and Lori Yarvis, this guide includes information on federal, New York State, and New York City employment laws. The publication also includes a discussion on how to develop personnel policies and manuals, hiring and firing, treatment of independent contractors, and employees and antidiscrimination laws—available through Lawyers Alliance for New York, (212) 219-1800.

Build a Better Staff, Volume III: Legal Issues and Your Nonprofit. This workbook provides coverage of discrimination and other issues of concern to nonprofits. It includes information on the Americans with Disabilities Act, sexual harassment, civil rights, etc.— available through Aspen Publishers, (800) 638-8437.

Personnel Policies for Nonprofit Organizations. This 1993 manual includes sample policies that illustrate different approaches used by nonprofit organizations in developing personnel policies— available through the Center for Nonprofit Management, Dallas, (214) 826-3470.

Nonprofit Personnel Policies Manual. This 1993 manual by John Gillis and Jamie Whaley offers sample policies covering a wide range of topics, including discipline, staff policy, code of ethics, and nondiscrimination—available through Aspen Publishers, (800) 638-8437.

Personnel Policies and Procedures for Nonprofit Organizations. This book by Michael E. Burns and Jeremy Landau provides the descriptions, rationale, sample policies, and procedures to create a personnel manual—available through the Development and Technical Assistance Center, (203) 772-1345.

Personnel Guide for Nonprofits. This workbook covers many aspects of the employer-employee relationship, including information on hiring practices, compensation, personnel policies, and discrimination—available through the Philadelphia Volunteer Lawyers for the Arts, (215) 545-3385.

How to Write Job Descriptions. This 1992 book by Louise Samson describes the process of developing job descriptions and includes a glossary of 200 terms and a checklist for job-description writing—available from Abbott, Langer & Associates, (708) 672-4200.

"How to Plan for Volunteer & Staff Success." Marlene Wilson authored this audio and videotape package that includes information on designing job descriptions, reaching objectives and ranking and organizing job responsibilities—available through Volunteer Management Associates, (800) 944-1470.

"1996 Wage & Benefit Survey of Northern California Nonprofit Organizations." Published by the Management Center, this survey was used by ARDI in the wage-and-benefit analysis. The Management Center has included a section on 1995–1996 state and federal personnel statutes—available through the Management Center, (415) 362-9735 or (800) 349-6627.

TRAINING AND CONSULTATION SOURCES

The following organizations offer information services, publications, and training and/or consultation on a variety of human resources topics.

- Nonprofit Risk Management Center, 1001 Connecticut Avenue, NW, Suite 900, Washington, D.C. 20036, (202) 785-3891
- American Compensation Association, P.O. Box 29312, Phoenix, AZ 85038-9312, (602) 951-9191
- American Management Association, 135 West 50th Street, New York, NY 10020, (212) 586-8100
- Society of Human Resource Management, 606 N. Washington Street, Alexandria, VA 22314-1997, (703) 548-3440
- American Society of Association Executives, 1575 Eye Street, NW, Washington, D.C. 20005-1168, (202) 626-2723

ARDI's 1996 "Management and Leadership Resources for Nonprofits" directory also includes a reference section that profiles over 200 organizations that provide consulting and technical assistance to nonprofit organizations. ARDI is presently surveying nearly 10,000 organizations and individuals that provide management and leadership assistance to nonprofits. The survey data will be compiled in an on-line database of assistance providers that will include contact and in-depth information on management expertise and services, delivery systems, geographic service area, and client and provider demographics. This database will be available on-line by the spring of 1998 at http//www.ardi.org.

For-profit consulting firms specializing in compensation management are cited in the bibliography.

Appendix A

NONPROFIT MANAGEMENT AND LEADERSHIP TAXONOMY

Advocacy

All communication and actions intended to build awareness, understanding, and support for the mission of a nonprofit organization or for the nonprofit sector itself. Advocacy methods include, but are not limited to, lobbying public officials, education and information directed either to a specific audience or to the general public, and community networking.

- General
- Lobbying
- Public Awareness
- Community Networking
- Other

Ethics

Rules or standards of conduct. Includes ethical decision making, behavior, and general and specific aspects of ethics related to nonprofit organization management and leadership.

- General
- Behavior

- Decision Making
- Special Nonprofit Management and Leadership Issues
- Other

Evaluation

Responsibilities, methods, and procedures for evaluation of a nonprofit organization and its component parts.

- General
- Models
- Procedures
- Responsibilities
- Other

Financial Management

Financial planning and budgeting, investments, accounting, payroll, taxes, cash management, annual government filings, reporting and analysis, internal controls, risk management, audits, and insurance.

- General
- Accounting/Reporting
- Auditing
- Budgeting
- Government Filing Requirements
- Investments
- Risk Management and Insurance
- Taxes
- Other

General Leadership

Information on leadership generally and on special issues related to leadership of nonprofit organizations, including philanthropy and volunteerism, trends affecting specific service types of nonprofit organizations, and leadership roles of managers and board members.

General Management

Information covering management generally and special issues related to managing nonprofit organizations.

Governance

General information on governance of nonprofit organizations and the roles, responsibilities, composition, and organization of nonprofit boards of directors.

- General
- Composition
- Organization
- Responsibilities
- Roles
- Other

Human Resource Management

The management and development of people as a resource. Includes administrative systems, policies, compensation, recruitment and employment, organization, and development of both paid staff members and volunteers.

- General
- Administrative Systems
- Compensation
- Employment and Career Search
- Interpersonal
- Organization
- Policies
- Recruitment
- Volunteer Management
- Other

Information Systems

Gathering and handling of recorded information. Includes planning for and establishing a management information system and its computer support, as well as employment of other technologies.

- General
- Computer Hardware
- Computer Software
- On-Line Resources
- Other Technologies
- Systems Planning
- Other

Legal

Information on laws and regulations pertaining to nonprofit corporate or other legal status, tax exemption, personnel, foundations, antitrust issues, copyright, charitable solicitations, liability, and other specialized concerns of nonprofit management.

- General
- Charitable solicitation
- Copyright
- Nonprofit Corporation, Organization, and Operations
- Personnel
- Private Foundations
- Tax Exemption
- Other

Marketing

Market research, product development, packaging and distribution, pricing, promotion, sales, public and community relations, and communications.

- General
- Packaging and Distribution
- Product Development
- Promotion and Media
- Public and Community Relations
- Research
- Sales
- Other

Operations Management

The management of resources to produce products and services. Includes general information on operations management, forecasting, facilities planning and management, office administration, capacity, scheduling systems, inventory control and purchasing, quality control, and multiple locations.

- General
- Capacity
- Facilities Planning and Management
- Forecasting
- Inventory Control/Purchasing
- Office Administration
- Quality Control
- Scheduling Systems
- Other

Organization, Design, and Structure

Information on starting a nonprofit organization, the design of organizational structures, affiliations and collaborations, mergers, and relationships between organizations or organizational units.

- General
- Affiliations
- Collaborations
- Design
- Mergers
- Multiple Related Organizations
- Start-up
- Other

Planning

Needs assessment; long-range, strategic and annual plans; roles in planning; and planning for specific types of services.

- General
- Implementation
- Needs Assessment
- Program
- Roles
- Types of Plans
- Other

Resource Development

Organizing and planning for resource development and all categories of fund raising, including grants, individual contributions, special events, and in-kind donations. Also covers other sources of funds, including earned income, investment income, and loans. (Recruiting volunteers is under Human Resource Development.)

- General
- Capital Campaigns
- Earned Income
- Grants
- Individual Contributions
- In-Kind Donations
- Loans
- Planned Giving and Bequests
- Prospect Research
- Special Events
- Other

Appendix B

NEW LEGISLATION

What You Need to Know for Your Organization*

During July and August of 1996, the President signed several bills that included provisions which may affect your nonprofit organization. These changes, outlined below, may significantly alter the benefits you are offering your employees.

401(k) Plans

In the past, tax exempt organizations could not have a 401(k) plan unless it was established prior to July 2, 1986. The new legislation has changed that. Now, tax exempt organizations may maintain cash or deferred arrangements described as Section 401(k) plans. This provision will be effective for plan years beginning after Dec. 31, 1996. State and local governments, however, will

*The article is reprinted from *Nonprofit Agendas*, February/March 1997, with permission of Kimberly K. Higgins, Partner, Bondi & Co. LLP, CPAs, Denver, CO, phone (303) 799-6826.

still be prohibited from having 401(k) plans unless they had adopted one before May 6, 1986.

401(k) plans are qualified plans containing a cash or deferred arrangement—employees can elect to have a portion of their salaries that would have been paid in cash deferred through payment to the qualified plan. The amount contributed to the qualified plan is called an elective contribution and, in general, these contributions are not included in the employee's taxable income for the year in which they are made. Also, earnings on the amounts contributed are not taxed until they are distributed— presumably for retirement. 401(k) plans may be stand-alone plans (permitting elective contributions only), or they may also permit other types of employer contributions and voluntary employee contributions. 401(k) plans have been popular for years as a tax-savings and retirement-planning vehicle for employees.

SIMPLE Plans

The law also creates a new kind of pension plan, the Savings Incentive Match Plan for Employees (SIMPLE). A SIMPLE plan allows employees to make elective contributions to the plan. This type of plan can only be adopted by employers with no more than 100 employees, who each received at least $5,000 in compensation from the employer the preceding year and do not maintain any other employer-sponsored retirement plan.

SIMPLE retirement plans allow for elective contributions to be made to an IRA for employees along with either matching contributions or non-elective contributions to be made by employers. To relieve the administrative burden on employers, SIMPLE plans are generally exempted from the nondiscrimination rules that apply to qualified plans; the top-heavy-plan rules do not apply; and the usual plan reporting requirements are reduced. SIMPLE plans will be effective for tax years beginning after Dec. 31, 1996. The addition of 401(k) plans and SIMPLE retirement plans will greatly improve benefits plan offerings for nonprofits and will help employees with tax and retirement planning.

Other Provisions Affecting Nonprofits

For tax years beginning after Dec. 31, 1995, 403(b) rules have been amended to allow employees to enter into more than one salary-reduction agreement in any taxable year. Under the new law, the rules applicable to 401(k) plans will determine the frequency that a salary reduction agreement may be entered into by participants in a 403(b) plan. The compensation to which the agreement applies and the ability to revoke the agreement will also be determined by these rules.

Also, for years beginning after Dec. 31, 1995, if employees make elective deferrals to 403(b) plans that exceed the $9,500 limit, the plan itself will not lose its tax-favored status. Instead, the problem will fall with the individual annuity contract.

For tax years beginning after Dec. 31, 1996, the dollar limits on deferrals under Section 457 Deferred Compensation Plans (whichever is less, $7,500 or one-third of current compensation) will be indexed for inflation.

The long-awaited intermediate sanctions provisions were also enacted on July 31, 1996, under the Taxpayer Bill of Rights 2. These provisions impose excise tax penalties on individuals deemed to have received inurement, or excess benefits, from exempt entities—rather than the entity itself losing its tax exempt status. The penalties, which start at 25% of the amount of the excess benefit, apply initially only to 501(c)(3) and (4) organizations, although we anticipate that these penalties will ultimately be applied to a broader range of nonprofits. The penalties apply to the officers, directors, trustees, and others who exercise substantial influence over the organization's business. These penalties will require nonprofits to place careful emphasis on documenting compensation decisions.

How Will These Changes Affect You?

As always, rules and regulations are associated with the new legislation, so it is critical that you fully understand all implications prior to putting any new policies into effect. Please call us at (303) 799-6826 if you have any questions or would like further information on any of these items.

Appendix C

EXECUTIVE COMPENSATION BY CHARITABLE ORGANIZATIONS: A LEGAL PERSPECTIVE*

by David G. Samuels

Charitable organizations are permitted, pursuant to both federal and state law, to pay "reasonable" compensation to their executives. Such compensation is ordinarily fixed by the charity's board of directors, which should ideally be independent and function at arm's length.

Excessive or unwarranted compensation can be deemed "private inurement" by the Internal Revenue Service and can threaten the tax-exempt status of the organization; such excessive compensation could also result in the imposition of civil damages and injunctive relief in certain states against the members of the board or the recipient of the unwarranted compensation.

Furthermore, the payment to executives of charitable groups has been subject to scrutiny by the donating public, and what is perceived by the public as overly generous compensation can result in a decrease in contributions even where the compensation is not illegal.

Boards, executive directors, and the legal advisors of organizations in the burgeoning nonprofit sector must be familiar with the federal and state laws governing compensation for executives

*Portions of this material originally appeared in the *New York Law Journal*. Used with permission.

and other employees, to assure that the board members do not run afoul of the maze of regulatory requirements or otherwise breach their fiduciary duties in fixing such compensation.

At the same time, board members and their legal counsel must be sensitive to increasing public scrutiny of executive compensation, particularly in the wake of William Aramony's forced departure as president of the United Way of America in 1992. Mr. Aramony's departure was precipitated by "reports that he had misused the charity's money to pay for vacations, luxury apartments, and other benefits for himself and his teen-age girlfriend, and his earnings of $463,000 in salary and benefits took some by surprise" (1).

Public Concern

Recently, the *New York Times* reported that "[t]op executives of the largest charities and foundations often earn $200,000 a year or more, and their salaries continue to grow even as the pay scale of these groups comes under increased scrutiny" (2). Citing a survey made public by *The Chronicle of Philanthropy*, which relied in part on a survey by the accounting firm of Ernst & Young, the *Times* also pointed out that "the majority of executives at nonprofits earn far less," and the majority of nonprofit groups have annual budgets of less than $500,000 (3).

"If Congress succeeds in its efforts to cut the federal budget by slashing social service spending, much of which is provided through government grants to religious and other charitable organizations, the budgets of many such charities are likely to become even smaller" (4). It is the compensation paid to certain executives at larger charities, including (in particular) United Way of America, that has galvanized public interest in this issue.

In April 1995, several years after Mr. Aramony left United Way, he and two other top-level executives of the charity were convicted of looting more than $500,000 from the organization's coffers. Mr. Aramony was "convicted on 25 felony counts of heading a conspiracy to defraud United Way in order to subsi-

dize a high-flying lifestyle that included lavish European vacations and gambling trips" (5). In the midst of the trial, and shortly
before the verdict, the New York Attorney General filed suit
against Mr. Aramony and one of the other former executives,
accusing them, in a civil complaint that essentially overlapped
the criminal action, of mismanaging and wasting United Way's
corporate assets and breaching their fiduciary duties as officers
of the charity (6). Significantly, however, no criminal or civil
charges have been filed by any federal or state agency against
Mr. Aramony, the United Way of America, or its board of directors with respect to the $463,000 in annual compensation paid to
Mr. Aramony.

This high level of compensation was a source of much of the
controversy concerning the United Way in particular and executive compensation in general. However, the salary paid to Mr.
Aramony and other United Way employees has long been a
matter of public record, since United Way of America is required
by state and federal regulations to file its annual financial reports.
Mr. Aramony's compensation was fixed in an employment contract negotiated at arm's length with an independent board of
directors, consisting largely of the top executives of a number of
major corporations. His compensation was considerably less than
the annual compensation earned by the vast majority of these
board members, and Mr. Aramony had a wide range of responsibilities with respect to a large, vibrant organization, which had
achieved considerable growth under his tenure.

Statutory Framework

The concept of "Private Inurement" is central to any analysis of
executive compensation by tax-exempt charitable organizations,
which are eligible for tax-exempt status pursuant to Section
501(c)(3) of the Internal Revenue Code. If they achieve such status, they obtain a dual benefit not available to other types of tax-
exempt organizations: In addition to being freed of the obligations to pay income taxes, they have the added advantage of

obtaining contributions from individuals who can deduct such contributions from their income tax obligations, thereby providing a powerful incentive to make such contributions.

To obtain and retain 501(c)(3) status, charitable groups must function in such a manner that "no part of the net earnings . . . inures to the private shareholder or individual. . . ." It has long been held by the federal courts that "the payment of reasonable salaries by an allegedly tax-exempt organization does not result in the increment of net earnings to the benefit of private individuals" (7). If an executive's salary is found to be excessive and unreasonable, inurement would result so as to disqualify the organization as tax-exempt (8).

Whether salaries are reasonable is a question of fact, and "an organization's net earnings may inure to the benefit of private individuals in ways other than by the actual distribution of dividends or payments of excessive salaries" (9).

As a practical matter, inurement is "most likely to arise when an 'insider' relationship exists between the person benefited and the organization. Generally, an organization's officers, directors, founders, and their families are considered insiders" (10). The Internal Revenue Service considers factors relating to the employee, the organization, and the compensation itself in determining whether compensation is excessive and therefore constitutes prohibited private inurement (11).

Among the factors relating to the employee are the arm's length relationship between the employee and employer, the extent of domination of the charity by the founder of a particular family (which is obviously viewed as negative), the availability of comparable services from a third party, the nature of the employee's background and experience, the employee's contribution to the organization's success, and the time devoted by the employee to the job.

Factors relating to the organization include the salary scale of others in the same line of business, the size of the organization, the salary scale for employees generally, and the amount of the organization's income devoted to compensation.

Factors related to the compensation itself include the criteria for compensation (which should be spelled out clearly by the board, laying out the person's duties, responsibilities, and measures of success in the position), the existence or absence of abrupt increases in compensation (which, if abrupt, are viewed with suspicion), whether a salary is fixed many years in advance (which would suggest control by the employee over the organization), and the existence of records by which the organization can substantiate the duties performed and the salary paid.

While the IRS has the power to deny or revoke tax-exempt status in instances of private inurement, such drastic remedy is rarely imposed. However, the IRS now has another tool at its disposal when punishing nonprofit organizations: Intermediate Sanctions.

Intermediate Sanctions

At the urging of the Department of the Treasury, a bill which President Clinton signed into law provides the Internal Revenue Service with new and increasingly flexible sanctions "to curb financial abuse among charities and other tax-exempt groups, which have grown rapidly and with little regulation." In addition, the new legislation is designed to make it easier for the public to obtain copies of the informational tax returns filed by charities with the IRS.

This new legislation affords the IRS the ability to impose more appropriate, and less draconian, remedies than the ones previously available to it. Rather, as a practical matter, "this possibility is often more properly used as a tool to persuade exempt organizations' boards of directors to tighten their oversight and control of compensation" (12). Nonprofit boards, executive directors, and their legal counsel should become familiar with this new legislation, as well as with the range of federal and state laws governing compensation for executives and other employees.

This widely anticipated legislation, which has been enacted in the aftermath of William Aramony's forced departure as president of the United Way, is likely to result in increased scrutiny by the IRS of executive compensation and in more vigorous and frequent enforcement of the Code's prohibition of private inurement by charitable organizations. Marcus Owens, director of the IRS's Exempt Organization division, stated, "We only had an atomic bomb before. . . . Now we'll have less severe weapons."

The statute permits the IRS to impose an excise tax "equal to 25 percent of the excess benefit" on a "disqualified person" with respect to each "excess benefit transaction." Furthermore, in any case where the 25 percent tax is imposed on a disqualified person "and the excess benefit involved in such transactions not corrected within the taxable period, there is hereby imposed a tax equal to 200 percent of the excess benefit involved," with such additional amounts to be paid by the disqualified person.

An understanding of the terms "disqualified person," "excess benefit transaction," and "excess benefit" is obviously crucial in analyzing the new statute. An "excess benefit transaction" is defined by the statute as "any transaction in which an economic benefit is provided by an applicable tax-exempt organization directly or indirectly to or for the use of any disqualified person if the value of the economic benefit provided exceeds the value of the consideration (including the performance of services) received for providing such benefit." This definition is consistent with the concept of private inurement. It is well-settled that "the payment of reasonable salaries by an allegedly tax-exempt organization does not result in the inurement of new earnings to the benefit of private individuals."

Having defined an "excess benefit transaction" in a manner consistent with the concept of private inurement, the statute then defines an "excess benefit" as merely the excess benefit paid to such a disqualified person. The concept of a disqualified person, which is well known to individuals familiar with the law applicable to private foundations, has now been applied in the new statute in somewhat different form to charities which are not private foundations.

In essence, a "disqualified person" is an insider or someone with a particular relationship to an insider of a charitable organization. The new statute defined a "disqualified person" as a person who, with respect to any transaction of the organization, "was, at any time during the five-year period ending on the date of such transaction, in a position to exercise substantial influence over the affairs of the organization." This definition of a "disqualified person" also applies to family members of the individual who is in a position to exercise control.

The strength and flexibility of the IRS's new enforcement authority is underscored by its power to impose a 200 percent tax on any disqualified person who is involved in an excess benefit transaction, where the IRS has imposed a 25 percent tax on such a person and the excess benefit is not corrected within the taxable period. The term "taxable period" is defined as "the period beginning with the date on which the transaction occurs and ending on the earliest of the date of mailing a notice of deficiency or the assignment of the tax."

The term "correction" is defined, with respect to an excess benefit transaction, as "undoing the excess benefit to the extent possible, and taking any additional measures necessary to place the organization in a financial position not worse than that in which it would be if the disqualified person were dealing under the highest fiduciary standards." Thus, a disqualified person whom the IRS finds to have received an excess benefit should promptly correct the problem, or risk being subject to a larger confiscatory tax.

The IRS's authority to combat excessive compensation by charitable organizations is further strengthened by a provision enabling it to impose a 10 percent excise tax on any "organization manager" who has participated in an excess benefit transaction. The tax on an organization manager may only be imposed in instances where a 25 percent tax is being imposed on a disqualified person involved in an excess benefit transaction. The 10 percent tax is computed as a percentage of the excess benefit received by the disqualified person, and will be paid by any manager who participated in the excess benefit transaction.

In addition to its intermediate sanctions provisions, the statute is designed to facilitate the individual's efforts to obtain copies of an organization's Form 990, which is the informational tax return filed each year by most tax-exempt organizations (with religious organizations and smaller organizations exempt from the filing requirement). Specifically, the new statute requires that, during the three-year period commencing with the filing of an organization's Form 990, a copy of such return "shall be made available by such organization for inspection during business hours by any individual at the principal office of such organizations" and at regional or district offices of such organizations which have three or more employees at the regional or district office.

In addition, copies of the return must be provided upon request, subject only to reproduction fees. The penalty for willful failure to allow public inspection of the returns has been increased from $1000 to $5000, and the penalties imposed on exempt organizations which fail to file complete and timely annual returns have been increased. In light of the requirements imposed on charities to report the compensation paid to their highest paid executives in their Form 990's, the enhanced availability of these returns will make it easier for the contributing public to scrutinize the compensation paid by the charities to which the public might consider making contributions.

Conclusion

The issues of reasonable compensation and private inurement will continue to be of great concern to the IRS as well as the Department of the Treasury, as can be seen by their support of the recently enacted intermediate sanctions legislation, which permits the IRS to seek intermediate sanctions through new excise taxes aimed at abuses involving private inurement and reasonable compensation.

In addition to concerns about federal or state enforcement, attorneys counseling not-for-profit charitable organizations should encourage their board members and executives to remain sensitive to public concerns about the salaries paid to their top executives, while also permitting such executives to earn a decent living and thereby attracting superior executive talent to the nonprofit sector.

References

1. *NY Times*, Sept. 5, 1995, p. 12, col. 1.

2. *NY Times*, Sept. 5, 1995, p. 12, col. 1.

3. *NY Times*, Sept. 5, 1995, p. 12, col. 1.

4. See *NY Times* column by Peter Steinels, Oct. 28, 1995, p. 11, column 3.

5. *The Chronicle of Philanthropy*, April 2, 1995, p. 30.

6. *NY Times*, March 16, 1995, p. B12, col. 6.

7. Founding Church of Scientology, 412 F2d at 1200.

8. Mabee Petroleum Corp. v. U.S., 203 F2d 872 (5th Cir, 1953).

9. Founding Church of Scientology, 412 F2D at 1200.

10. "Reasonable Compensation" by Jean Wright and Jay H. Rotz, p. 195, Exempt Organization Continuing Professional Education Technical Instruction for 1993 (not to be "used or cited as authority for setting or sustaining a technical position").

11. Id. At 201–209.

12. Id. At 191.

Appendix D

The next article further elaborates on the intermediate sanctions and is reprinted with permission of James E. Rocco, James E. Rocco & Associates. Copyright *Philanthropy Monthly*, 1996.

NEW LEGISLATION INCREASES SCRUTINY OF NOT-FOR-PROFIT EXECUTIVE COMPENSATION

by Larry F. Beers

On July 30, 1996, President Clinton signed into law the Taxpayer Bill of Rights 2 (H.R. 2337). This Legislation amends "the Internal Revenue Code of 1986 to provide for increased taxpayer protections." Included in its provisions is the creation of a Taxpayer Advocate's office within the Internal Revenue Service to assist taxpayers in resolving problems with the IRS, [to] identify areas in which taxpayers have problems in dealing with the IRS, and [to] propose changes in or administrative practices of the IRS to mitigate problems. The law also includes language intended to ensure that executive compensation in not-for-profit organizations is not excessive.

Since Jim and Tammy Faye Bakker's ouster from PTL Ministries and the departure of William Aramony from the United Way, not-for-profit executive compensation has been questioned by the public and lawmakers. Certainly, there have been some examples of excess; however, most charitable organizations are cognizant of the public scrutiny this issue faces and the potential impact on donor relations and their contributions. Faced with the demands of running mission-driven organizations with strong business acumen, not-for-profits are increasingly on the horns of a dilemma: how to compensate executives at a level that is comparable to their experience and value, while recognizing the constraints of their budgets and the popular perception that "not-for-profit" means "low pay."

The Taxpayer Bill of Rights 2 increases the level of scrutiny on how not-for-profit executives are compensated. Subtitle B, 1311 of the law establishes "excise taxes for failure by certain charitable organizations to meet certain qualification requirements." A close reading of this and subsequent sections reveals that the "failure to meet certain qualification requirements" means simply that executives are *too well* compensated. Or, as the bill puts it, "the value of the economic benefit provided exceeds the value of the consideration (including the performance of services)." Such wording makes clear that the term "economic benefit" applies not only to base salary, but to benefits and perquisites offered to an executive of a charitable organization during their employment.

The law also specifies that "excess benefit transactions" can be called into question "at any time during the five-year period ending on the date of such transaction." Clearly the intent of this provision is to minimize the "gold" in executive parachutes. Both lump-sum and extended payout severance packages or buy-outs for executives at charitable organizations will be subject to review and must be kept within reason.

The penalties are steep: the "disqualified person" who is recipient of the "excess benefit transaction" is subject to an excise tax of 25% of the excess benefit paid, as is any member of his or her immediate family who might alternatively be appointed recipient of the benefit. If the situation is not corrected within the taxable period in which the "transaction occurred" (i.e., the excess benefit is returned or repaid), an additional tax of 200% of the excess must be paid by the recipient or family member.

The sanctions to not stop there: any "officers, directors, or trustees" who participated in or approved the "excess benefit transaction" are subject to a penalty of 10% of the excess benefit paid, to a maximum of $10,000. While this penalty is assessed "jointly and severally" among those involved, compensation committees must beware that their decisions might expose them, the executives they direct, and the organizations they represent to significant liability.

The law does not provide an escape clause for those directors, officers, and trustees who participate in making compensation decisions for not-for-profit executives—if the excess benefit transaction is not willful, or if it is due to "reasonable cause."

Mr. Beers is a Consulting Associate with James E. Rocco Associates, a consulting practice based in Purchase, New York, specializing in not-for-profit human resources and compensation consulting. The practice has done extensive work in the area of executive compensation, including design of compensation packages and incentive plans.

Glossary

Affirmative action   Process for assuring equal opportunity and nondiscrimination by an employer or program provider to ensure equal access to employment and program services.

Average   The sum of all salary data divided by the number of salaries entered.

Bonuses   Awards paid at senior management's discretion to acknowledge outstanding individual job performance or to encourage special activities.

Bookkeeper   The person responsible for maintaining the accounting records and files.

Budget   Financial plan or action for future periods.

Clerk-typist   Performs clerical duties, answers incoming calls, places outgoing calls, receives visitors and directs to the appropriate person or office. This person typically performs a variety of clerical support and public relations functions under the direct supervision of the office manager.

COMP KEY   1990 study conducted by ARDI that revealed how nonprofit compensation compared with government and for-profit compensation; also reported on national work force, nonprofit, and employment trends.

Controller   The executive responsible for directing the organization's accounting practices and procedures, maintaining financial records, and preparing financial management reports and procedures. Duties include supervision of all accounting and budget functions, collection and analyses of statistical and accounting information, and other activities that impact the fiscal stability and effective operation of the organization.

Dependent life insurance The organization offers life insurance options to family members.

Department director Executive responsible for coordinating, implementing, and directing the efforts in one particular area or division of an organization or agency. Works with the executive director and supervises the activities of other professionals to achieve the organization's goals.

Deputy director The executive responsible for coordinating, implementing, and directing policies and procedures assigned to the executive director.

Direct compensation Pay received in the form of cash or cash equivalents; wage and salaries.

Disability The organization offers a combination plan including long- and short-term disability insurance.

Employee One who performs services for compensation and whose working conditions are set by the employer. Everyone who works for an organization, including owners or partners, full-time and part-time employees.

Excess benefit The economic value of a benefit provided to a disqualified person by a nonprofit organization.

Executive director An employee of an organization who is assigned the principal responsibility for administering the organization.

Flexible benefits plan Allows an employer to offer a variety of benefit options for employees, such as health, dental, vision, term-life, disability, prepaid legal services, child care, and medical or dental reimbursements. These options are selected and paid for by the employee with prepaid tax dollars through salary reductions.

401(k) plans A profit-sharing or stock bonus plan wherein an employee may choose to be paid in cash or through having the funds placed in a trust under the plan.

403(b) plan   Tax-deferred annuity plan for retirement for employees of tax-exempt organizations.

Fund raiser   One who is employed or retained to assist a nonprofit organization in the raising of funds, conventionally in the form of "contributions" and "grants."

Gain sharing   Awards representing employees' share of the gains of actual results achieved above preestablished operational goals. The "gains" are paid in the form of short-term cash incentive awards when the goals are exceeded.

Indirect compensation   Pay received in the form of benefits or services.

Individual incentives   Cash awards to recognize the achievement of predetermined performance objectives; an incentive award is usually calculated as a percentage of salary range midpoint.

Innovative compensation practices   Encompasses cash compensation, recognition, and benefit plan options.

Innovative Compensation Practices in the Nonprofit Sector   Reported in this book, study by ARDI conducted in 1995, included trends, surveys, and case studies of nonprofit organizations that had implemented innovative compensation practices.

IOMA   Institute of Management Administration.

Intermediate sanctions   Federal penalties, structured as excise taxes, which are imposed on disqualified persons who engage in excess benefit transactions with applicable tax-exempt organizations, and on organizational directors and managers who approve such transactions.

HMO (Health maintenance organization)   Plans that include a variety of coverage and payment options. HMOs consist of a network of hospitals and physicians, and patients must see a designated primary care physician and/or attend a designated hospital within this network.

Human resource management The management and development of people as a resource, includes compensation, employment and career search, interpersonal, organization, policies, recruitment, volunteer management.

Life insurance Includes a variety of plan options, but typically refers to a basic group life plan.

Market pricing of jobs Compensation levels set in relation to compensation for similar jobs in other organizations.

Major medical Plans that pay benefits for a wide range of medical expenses, including inpatient/outpatient services, prescriptions, wellness benefits, and typically some form of life insurance coverage.

Median The middle number in a series, or the level below which 50 percent of the sample falls, i.e., the 50th percentile.

Nonprofit Management and Leadership Taxonomy Classification system developed by ARDI, which allows people to understand, in an organized system, the functions and subfunctions that comprise this field of management.

Nonprofit organization Organization created and operated for what the applicable law (federal tax law) regards as a charitable purpose.

Office manager The person responsible for general office services, including the supervision of office personnel, scheduling workload, maintenance of equipment, and ordering supplies.

Organization manager The paid staff leader of an organization.

Organization structure or infrastructure Definition of functions, positions, and capabilities within an organization.

Paid employees Includes paid personnel who perform work for pay on a regular ongoing basis for an organization.

Pension plan   One providing for definitely determinable retirement benefits over a period of years for participants and their beneficiaries. A tax-qualified plan must be in writing, be established by an employer, be communicated to employees, be a permanent rather than a temporary program, and must exist for the exclusive benefit of covered employees and their beneficiaries.

Preferred Provider Organization   Similar to an HMO in that there is a network of hospitals and physicians. However, patients are not required to see a designated physician or attend a network hospital, although cost savings are realized when patients stay within the network.

Private inurement   The doctrine that causes a nonprofit organization to lose or be denied their tax-exempt status where the organization is operated for the private gain of an insider.

Salary   The base annual salary excluding bonuses and other short-term incentives.

Secretary   Performs a variety of clerical and typing duties and provides support to one or several professionals or managers.

75th percentile   The level *below* which 75 percent of the sample falls, or the level *above* which 25 percent of the sample falls.

Skill-based pay   Employees are paid according to the skills they have or acquire, not the job they hold.

SERP   Supplemental Employee Retirement Program. Restores benefits to top executives not covered under qualified retirement programs.

Supplemental life insurance   The organization offers the option of obtaining coverage in addition to the regular group plan. Almost always paid for by the employee and usually offered to executive-level employees only.

Supplemental executive plans   These are special plans that are typically offered to managerial-level employees. These plans allow the employee additional retirement or investment options, but usually not additional funds for these purposes.

Team or group incentive   Same as individual incentive except awards are made based on achievement of team or group predetermined performance objectives.

25th percentile   The level below which 25 percent of the survey sector falls.

Work unit   Includes person or group of people to whom the board of directors of a nonprofit organization delegates work. Forms may include, but not be limited to, committees, subcommittees, task forces, and ad hoc assignments.

Bibliography

Abbott, Langer & Associates, *Compensation in Nonprofit Organizations, 9th Edition*. Crete, IL: Abbott, Langer & Associates, 1996.

Abbot, Langer & Associates, *Compensation of Chief Executive Officers In Nonprofit Organizations, 9th Edition*. Crete, IL: Abbott, Langer & Associates, 1996.

Abowd, John M., "Does Performance-based managerial compensation affect corporate performance?," *Industrial and Labor Relations Review* 43 (February 1990).

Alvarado, Elliott I., "The Validity of Supplemental Pay Systems in Nonprofit Organizations," *Nonprofit Management and Leadership* 6 (3), 1996.

American Management Association, *Compensation & Benefits Review* (September/October 1996).

American Management Association, "Stingy Pay Raises," *HR Focus* 73 (August 1996).

Anthes, Earl W., and Jerry Cronin, editors, *Personnel Matters in the Nonprofit Organization*. Madison, WI: Society for Nonprofit Organizations, 1987.

Association of Washington Cities, *Washington City and County Employee Salary and Benefits Survey for 1996*. Olympia, WA: Association of Washington Cities, 1996.

Augustine, Lori, "Popular Staff Benefits," *Staff Leader* (June 1996).

Barbeito, Carol L., Ph.D., *COMP KEY Effective Compensation: A Key to Non-Profit Success*. Denver, CO: Applied Research and Development Institute International, 1990.

Beatty, Randolph P., and Edward J. Zajac, "Managerial incentives, monitoring, and risk bearing: A study of executive compensation, ownership, and board structure in initial public offerings," *Administrative Science Quarterly* 39 (June 1994).

Benjamin, Janice Y., and Marcia A. Manter, "How to Hold onto First Careerists," *Personnel Administrator* (September 1989).

Berglas, Steven, "When Money Talks, People Walk," *Inc.* (May) 1996.

Bildersee, Robert A., *Private Sector Retirement Plan Provisions of the Small Business Job Protection Act of 1996*. Morgan, Lewis & Bockius LLP, 1996.

Blum, Debra E., Paul Demko, Susan Gray, and Holly Hall, "Top Dollar for Charities' Top Leaders," *Chronicle of Philanthropy* 8 (23).

Bondi & Co. LLP, "New Legislation—What You need to Know for Your Organization," *Nonprofit Agendas: Managing a Nonprofit in a For-Profit World* (February/March 1997).

Bondi & Co. LLP, "Understanding Benefit Plan Compliance: Don't Put Yourself at Risk," *Nonprofit Agendas: Managing a Nonprofit in a For-Profit World* (February/March 1997).

Braden, Bradley R., and Stephanie L. Hyland, "Cost of employee compensation in public and private sectors,"*Monthly Labor Review* 116 (May 1993).

Braham, Jim, "A Rewarding Place to Work," *Industry Week* (September 1989).

Brenner, Lynn, "Crossing the Line," *CFO: The Magazine for Senior Financial Executives* 12 (October 1996).

Bureau of Labor Statistics, "BLS Reports on Employee Benefits in State and Local Governments, 1994," *Bureau of Labor Statistics* (On-line). Available: *http://www.stats.bls.gov/ebs2.toc.htm*.

Bureau of Labor Statistics, "Bureau of Labor Statistics Reports on

Employee Benefits in Small Private Industry Establishments, 1994," *Bureau of Labor Statistics* (On-line). Available: *http://www.stats.bls.gov/news.release/ebs.toc.htm.*

Bureau of Labor Statistics, "COMP2000," *Bureau of Labor Statistics* (On-line). Available *http://stats.bls.gov/comover.htm.*

Bureau of Labor Statistics, "Employee Benefits Survey," *Bureau of Labor Statistics* (On-line). Available: *http://www.stats.bls.gov/ebshome.htm.*

Bureau of Labor Statistics, "Occupational Outlook Handbook," *Bureau of Labor Statistics* (On-line). Available: *http://stats.bls.gov/oco/oco2003.htm.*

Bureau of National Affairs, "Non-Traditional Incentive Pay Programs," *Personnel Policies Forum Survey* (May 1991, No. 148).

Business & Legal Reports, Inc., *1996 Survey of Employee Benefits,* Madison, CT: Business & Legal Reports, Inc., 1996.

Business & Legal Reports, Inc., *1996 Survey of Exempt Compensation,* Madison, CT: Business & Legal Reports, Inc., 1996.

Business & Legal Reports, Inc., "Good News/Bad News: Job Protection Act Cuts Taxes, Hikes Minimum Wage," *What to Do about Personnel Problems* (October 1996, Issue 265).

Business & Legal Reports, Inc., "New Health Law Gives Workers 'Portable' Benefits, Affects All Employers with Coverage," *What to Do about Personnel Problems* (October 1996, Issue 265).

California Guide, *Collective Bargaining.* Sacramento, CA: California Guide, 1995.

Carrera, Nora, "Few minorities at non-profits," *Rocky Mountain News* (November 15, 1995).

Center for Management Assistance, *1995 Nonprofit Salary and Benefits Survey of the Greater Kansas City Area.* Kansas City, MO: Center for Management Assistance, 1995.

Colorado Municipal League, *Benchmark Employee Compensation Report.* Denver, CO: Colorado Municipal League, 1996.

Colorado Municipal League, *Management Compensation Report.* Denver, CO: Colorado Municipal League, 1996.

Council of State Government, *The Book of the States, 1996–97.* Lexington, KY: Council of State Government, 1996.

Craig, Jon, "More Options for Charity Pension Plans," *Chronicle of Philanthropy* 9 (10) 1997.

Crystal, Graef S., and Samuel J. Silberman, "Not-for-Profit Organizations Need Incentive Compensation," *Personnel Journal* (April 1986).

Cumming, Charles M., "Incentives That Really Do Motivate," *Compensation & Benefits Review* (May-June 1994).

Delaware Association of Nonprofit Agencies, *Delaware Nonprofit Wage & Benefit Survey, 1996 Edition.* Wilmington, DE: Delaware Association of Nonprofit Agencies, 1996.

Demko, Paul, Susan Gray, and Holly Hall, "Women Still Lag at the Top," *Chronicle of Philanthropy* 8 (23) 1996.

Deutsch, Claudia A., "It's Job, Not Benefits, for Women Executives," *Denver Post* (June 25, 1990).

Drucker, Peter, "Peter Drucker on the Non-profit Environment," *The Taft Non-profit Executive* 9 (3) 1989.

Duclaux, Denise, "Beyond Paychecks," *ABA Banking Journal* 88 (October 1996).

Dunaway, Tom, "Morale Coupons," *Training & Development* (May 1992).

Eclipse Publications Ltd., "Where to pitch your managers' pay," *IRS Employment Review* (July 1996, No. 612).

Ernst & Young LLP, 1995 Survey of New York Metropolitan Area Not-for-Profit Organizations, Compensation and Benefits, New York: Ernst & Young, 1996.

Ernst & Young LLP, *National Survey of Executive Compensation 4th Edition.* New York: Ernst & Young, 1990.

Ex Comp Service (ECS), *1995/1996, Top Management Report*, Rochelle Park, NJ: ECS, A Wyatt Data Services Company, 1996.

Fanning, Diedre, "Retirement: Does It Kill Executives?," *New York Times* (May 29, 1990).

Federal Employees News Digest, "1996 General Schedule Pay Tables by Locality," *Federal Employees News Digest*, 1996.

Filipczak, Bob, "Why No One Likes Your Incentive Program," *Training* (August 1993).

Florida League of Cities, *Cooperative Salary Survey, Group II: Cities with 10,000 to 49,000 Population.* Tallahassee, FL: Florida League of Cities, 1996.

Flynn, Gillian, "Look before you leap: Not all salary surveys are created equal," *Personnel Journal* 74 (June 1995).

Gemeinhardt, Gretchen, and Steve Werner, "Nonprofit salaries: What are you paying for?," *Nonprofit World* 13 (July/August 1995).

Goddard, Robert W., "Work Force 2000," *Personnel Journal* (February 1989).

Goldschmidt, Ellen, "Careers With a Conscience," *Self* (September 1989).

Greene, Stephen G., "The Challenge of Ethnic Diversity," *Chronicle of Philanthropy* 1 (19) 1989.

Haber, Jeffry A., "Bonus: Not a dirty Word," *Nonprofit World* 13 (March/April 1995).

Hall, Holly, "Charities' Bonus Debate," *Chronicle of Philanthropy* (July 1993).

Hay Group, Inc., *1996 Data Submission Materials, Customized Edition.* Philadelphia: Hay Group, Inc., 1996.

Hay Group, Inc., *1996 Job Matching Handbook, Job Families and Model Jobs.* Philadelphia: Hay Group, Inc., 1996.

Herman, Robert D., *The Jossey-Bass Handbook of Nonprofit Leader-*

ship and Management. San Francisco: Jossey-Bass Publishers, 1994.

Hodgkinson, Virginia Ann, Murray S. Weitzman, Stephen M. Noga, and Heather A. Gorski. *A Portrait of the Independent Sector*. Washington, D.C.: Independent Sector, 1993.

Hodgkinson, Virginia Ann, and Murray S. Weitzman, *Nonprofit Almanac 1996–1997: Dimensions of the Independent Sector*. San Francisco: Jossey-Bass Publishers, 1996.

Hohl, Karen L. "The Effects of Flexible Work Arrangements," *Nonprofit Management & Leadership* 7 (1) 1996.

Institute of Management and Administration (IOMA), "Effects of Gender on Compensation," *IOMA's Report on Salary Surveys*, 1996. (On-line). Available: *http://www.ioma.com/ioma/rss/index.html*.

Institute of Management and Administration (IOMA), "Exclusive IOMA Survey on Successful Ways to Control Compensation," *IOMA's Report on Salary Surveys*, 1996. (On-line). Available: *http://www.ioma.com/ioma/rss/index.html*.

Institute of Management and Administration (IOMA), "Survey Offers Early Estimates of 1997 Merit Pay Increases," *IOMA's Report on Salary Surveys*, 1996. (On-line). Available: *http://www.ioma.com/ioma/rss/index.html*.

Internal Revenue Service, "Where to pitch your managers' pay," *IRS Employment Review* (July 1996, No. 612).

Kanin-Lovers, Jill, "Market Pricing," *Journal of Compensation and Benefits* (March/April 1988).

Kanin-Lovers, Jill, "Salary Structure Design Can Be a Multipurpose Tool," *Journal of Compensation and Benefits* (May/June 1987).

Kanin-Lovers, Jill, "Total Compensation Analysis: A Broad Perspective," *Journal of Compensation and Benefits* (January/February 1989).

Kovach, Kenneth A., and John A. Pearce II, *Human Resources Strategic Mandates for the 1990s*. American Management Association, 1990.

Kurtz, Daniel L., "Fixing Nonprofit Executive Compensation," *VCG boardmember's FORUM*. New York: Volunteer Consulting Group, 1996.

Langer, Steven, "Latest salary survey," *Nonprofit World* 11 (3) 1993.

Langer, Steven, "Who's Being Paid What—And Why?," *Nonprofit World* 8 (6) 1990.

Lawler III, Edward E., *Merit Pay: An Obsolete Policy*, School of Business Administration, University of Southern California.

Lawler III, Edward E., *Pay for Performance: A Motivational Analysis*, School of Business Administration, University of Southern California.

Lawler III, Edward E., *The Design of Effective Reward Systems*, School of Business Administration, University of Southern California.

Lawler, Edward E., Lei Chang, and Gerald Ledford, "Who Uses Skill-Based Pay, and Why?" *Compensation & Benefits Review* (March-April 1993).

Lawler, Julia, "Cracks in the Glass Ceiling," *USA Today* (June 1990).

Lee, Tony, "Jobs Abound in the Growing Nonprofit Sector," *National Business Employment Weekly* (December 17, 1989).

Lee, Tony, "Non-profits Ready to Compete for Corporate Executives," *National Business Employment Weekly* (December 1988).

Leete, Laura, "Gender and Race Wage Differentials in the Nonprofit Sector," *work in progress*. Cleveland: Department of Economics, Weatherhead School of Management, Case Western Reserve University, 1995.

Mace, Don, and Eric Yoder, editors, *Federal Employees almanac, 1996, 43rd Edition*, Reston, VA: Federal Employees News Digest, Inc., 1996.

Management Center, *1996 Wage & Benefit Survey of Northern California Nonprofit Organizations*. San Francisco: The Management Center, 1996.

Massachusetts Municipal Personnel Association, *Municipal Salary Survey Benchmark Jobs 1989–1990*, Massachusetts Municipal Personnel Association, 1989.

Murawski, John, "Law Penalizing Lavish Nonprofit Salaries Causes Uncertainty," *Chronicle of Philanthropy* 8 (23) 1996.

National Association of State Personnel, *State Personnel Office: Rules and Functions*. Lexington, KY: National Association of State Personnel, 1996.

National Center for Charitable Statistics, *National Taxonomy of Exempt Entities, Mapping the Nonprofit Sector*. Washington, D.C.: Independent Sector.

National Center for Nonprofit Boards, "The Nonprofit Board's Guide to Chief Executive Compensation," *Board Member* 4 (5) 1995.

National Collaboration for Youth, *Salaries and Benefits in Youth Development Agencies 1996*. Washington D.C.: National Assembly of National Voluntary Health and Social Welfare Organizations, 1996.

Nebraska State Government, *Salary Survey*, Lincoln, NE: Personnel Division, 1996.

New York Compensation Association, "Alternative Rewards: Do They Work?" *Workforce Compensation*. New York: New York Compensation Association, 1993.

New York State Society of Certified Public Accountants, "Profiting from not-for-profits," *CPA Journal* 63 (3) March, 1993.

O'Connell, Brian, "Salaries in Nonprofit Organizations," *Nonprofit World* 10 (July/August, 1991).

Pennsylvania League of Cities and Municipalities, *1996 Salary and Benefits Survey*. Harrisburg, PA: Pennsylvania league of Cities and Municipalities, 1996.

Pratt, Nancy C., "CEOs reap unprecedented riches while employees' pay stagnates," *Compensation & Benefits Review* 28 (September/October 1996).

Rifkin, Jeremy, *The End of Work: The Decline of the Global Labor Force and The Dawn of the Post-Market Era*. New York: G.P. Putnam's Sons, 1995.

Rocco, James E., "How to Attract the Brightest People," *Nonprofit World* (May/June 1992).

Rocco, James E., "Incentive Plans Help Control Salary Costs," *The NonProfit Times* (May 1993).

Rocco, James E., *Innovative Compensation Practices in the Nonprofit Sector*. Denver, CO: Applied Research and Development Institute International, 1995.

Rocco, James E., "Making Incentive Plans Work for Nonprofits," *Nonprofit World* (July/August 1991).

Simms, Janet, "Disabled Making Inroads in the Workplace," *Rocky Mountain News* (November 15, 1995).

Society for Nonprofit Organizations, *Compensation in Nonprofit Organizations*. Madison, WI: Society for Nonprofit Organizations, 1989.

State of Oklahoma Compensation Division, *Oklahoma Merit System Classification and Compensation Plan*. Oklahoma City, OK: State of Oklahoma Compensation Division, 1996.

Steinberg, Richard, "Labor Economics and the Nonprofit Sector: A Literature Review," *Nonprofit and Voluntary Sector Quarterly* 19 (2) 1990.

Steinberg Richard, "Profits and Incentive Compensation in Nonprofit Firms," *Nonprofit Management & Leadership* 1 (2) 1990.

Stelluto, George L., and Deborah P. Klein, "Compensation trends into the 21st century," *Monthly Labor Review* 113 (February 1990).

Taft Group, "Association 'Think Tank' Considers Five Trends," *The Taft Non-profit Executive* 9 (6) 1990.

Taft Group, "The Greying American Workforce," *The Taft Non-profit Executive* 9 (7) 1989.

Taft Group, "A Futuristic Look, Trends in the Nonprofit Sector," *The Taft Non-profit Executive* 8 (11) 1989.

Technical Assistance Center, *1988 National Nonprofit Wage & Benefits Survey*. Denver, CO: Technical Assistance Center, 1988.

Tedford Jr., Gerald E., *The Effectiveness of Skill-Based Pay Systems*, Center for Effective Organizations, University of Southern California.

Tew, Jerry, "Leading the New Workforce," *Vision/Action* (5).

Texas Municipal League, *1996 Salaries and Fringe Benefits of Texas City Officials*. Austin, TX: Texas Municipal League, 1996.

Towers Perrin, *1997 Salary Management Planning Survey, Summary Report*. Rosslyn, VA: Towers Perrin, 1996.

Towers Perrin, *Compensation Survey of Management Positions in High Technology Companies*. Rosslyn, VA: Towers Perrin, 1995.

Towers Perrin, *1994 Management Compensation Report, Not-for-Profit Organizations*. Rosslyn, VA: Towers Perrin, 1994.

Towers Perrin, *1996 Management Compensation Report, Not-for-Profit Organizations*. Rosslyn, VA: Towers Perrin, 1996.

TPF & C, "The Power of Knowledge," *Salary Management* (1989 Issue 113).

U.S. Department of Labor, "Employee Benefits in Small Private Establishments, 1994," *Bulletin 2475*. Washington, D.C.: U.S. Department of Labor, 1996.

U.S. Department of Labor, "Employee Benefits Survey: A BLS Reader," *Bulletin 2459*. Washington, D.C.: U.S. Department of Labor, 1995.

U.S. Department of Labor, "Occupational Compensation Survey, National Summary, 1994," *Bulletin 2479*. Washington, D.C.: U.S. Department of Labor, 1996.

U.S. Department of Labor, "Occupational Compensation Survey:

Pay and Benefits," *Bulletin 3085-1*. Denver, CO: U.S. Department of Labor, 1996.

U.S. Department of Labor, "Occupational Compensation Survey: Pay Only West Palm Beach," *Bulletin 3085-10*. Boca Raton, FL: U.S. Department of Labor, 1996.

U.S. Department of Labor, "Employee Benefits in State and Local Governments, 1994," *Bulletin 2477*. Washington, D.C.: U.S. Department of Labor, 1996.

U.S. Department of Labor, "Employee Benefits in Medium and Large Private Establishments, 1993." *Bulletin 2456*. Washington, D.C.: U.S. Department of Labor, 1994.

U.S. Department of Labor, "Executive Summary," *Workforce 2000, Work and Workers for the 21st Century*. Washington, D.C.: U.S. Department of Labor, 1987.

Wein, Jay R., "Financial Incentives for Non-Profits," *Fund Raising Management* (September 1989).

William M. Mercer, Inc., "What the Rest of Us Make," *Mercury News* (On-line), 1996. Available: *http//www.sjmercury.com*.

Young, Dennis, *Performance and Reward in Nonprofit Organizations: Evaluation, Compensation, and Personnel Incentives*, Yale University—Program on Nonprofit Organizations, Working Paper No. 79, 1984.

Zajac, Edward J., and James D. Westphal, "Accounting for the explanations of CEO compensation: Substance and symbolism," *Administrative Science Quarterly* (June 1995).

Zehr, Mary Ann, "Same old salaries," *Foundation News* 34 (July/August 1993).

Index

affirmative action, 183
AMA (American Management Association), 22
American Compensation Association, 155
American Society of Association Executives, 155
ARDI (Applied Research and Development Institute), 3
  Advisory Committee, 80
  health benefits, xii
  low nonprofit executive and employee pay, xi–xii
"Association Executive Compensation Study, 9th Edition," 152

benefit plans, 101–108
  administration, 103
  board responsibility and employee involvement, 106–107
  changes in frequency of communications, 104–105
  communication methods, 104
  communications, 108
  definitions, 84
  issues, 106
  positive results, 105–108
  potential costs, 107
  survey overview, 101–102
  time, 108
  types, 102–103
benefits, 17–22
  cross-sector analysis and comparison results, 62–75
  cross-sector study, 31–75
  health, 17
  innovative, 63
  innovative compensation, 17–19
BNA (Bureau of National Affairs), 17
bonuses, 15, 82, 183
  paid to fund-raisers, 25–26

bookkeeper, 183
  alternate position titles, 53
  cross-sector median and average annual salaries, 54
  cross-sector salary analysis and comparison results, 53–55
  key findings, 54–55
  nonprofit median salaries by gender, 54
  position description, 53
  salary data, 54
403(b) plan, 72–73, 185
Braham, Jim, 19
budget, 183
Build a Better Staff, Volume III: Legal Issues and Your Nonprofit, 153
Bureau of Labor Statistics, 8

cash-compensation plans, 89–101
  administration, 95
  award as separate check, 94
  baseline used, 95
  cash/noncash as form of award, 94
  changes in employee problem solving and/or decision making, 97
  changes in frequency of communication, 96–97
  communication with plan participants, 95–96
  compensation basis, 93
  definitions, 82–83
  design implications, 92
  goal-level definitions, 99
  issues raised by, 99–101
  overview of survey results, 89–91
  participation, 99
  payouts as percentage of payroll, 92–93
  perceived favoritism, 100
  performance criteria, 95

cash-compensation plans *(continued)*
  positive results, 97–98
  qualitative goals, 100
  substitution for other compensation
    elements, 93
  target award payouts, 93–94
  teamwork and collaboration, 92
  time between end of plan and payout,
    92
  types and findings, 91–97
  unexpected occurrences, 100
Chang, Lei, 16
"Charities' Bonus Debate," 25
"Christian Ministries Salary Survey, 14th
  Edition," 152
clerk-typist, 183
  alternate position titles, 60
  cross-sector median and average
    salaries, 61
  cross-sector salary analysis and
    comparison results, 60–62
  key findings, 61–62
  nonprofit median salaries by gender,
    61
  position description, 60
  salary data, 61
"Colorado Springs Nonprofit Center
  Salary and Benefits Survey 1995,"
  152
compensation
  benefits of well-designed practices, 3–4
  competitive with other businesses, 14
  executive by charitable organizations,
    169–177
  first steps in establishing policy, 126–
    135
  gender differences, 14–15
  human resource management, 4
  low compensation for majority of
    workers, 23
  perceptions of high salaries, 23
  practices, 3
  program context, 4–5
  salaries as overhead cost, 23
  some salaries high, 23
  strategies, 14–16
Compensation & Benefits Review, 16
"Compensation in Nonprofit Organizations," 2
"Compensation in Nonprofit Organizations, 9th Edition," 151
*Compensation in Not-for-Profit Organiza-
  tions*, 149

"Compensation of Chief Executive
  Officers in Nonprofit Organizations,
  9th Edition," 151
compensation trends, 13–27
  components, 13
  cross-sector impacts on nonprofit
    sector, 22–27
  cross-sector practices, 14–22
  motivating employees, 22
COMP KEY, 183
"COMP KEY Effective Compensation: A
  Key to Non-Profit Success," xiii, 3
controller, 183
  alternate position titles, 51
  cross-sector median and average
    annual salaries, 51–52
  cross-sector salary analysis and
    comparison results, 50–53
  key findings, 52–53
  nonprofit median salaries by gender,
    51
  position description, 50
  salary data, 51
corporate in-kind contributions, 11
crossover employees and implementing
  compensation plans, 137
cross-sector benefits analysis and
  comparison results, 62–75
  health benefits, 64–66
  leave benefits, 68–71
  life and disability benefits, 66–68
  other benefits, 73–74
  retirement benefits, 71–73
cross-sector compensation impacts on
  nonprofit sector, 22–27
  adjusted profits, 26
  focus on performance, 24–25
  incentives and bonuses, 25
  innovative compensation, 25
  losing tax exempt status, 27
  low salaries, 23–24
  output-based incentives, 26
  penalties, 27
  tying incentive programs to indicators,
    26–27
  variable pay for executives, 24
cross-sector compensation trends, 14–22
  benefits, 17–22
  compensation strategies, 14–16
  executives and directors, 14
  gender differences, 14–15
  lump-sum payments, 15
  market pricing of jobs, 14

merit increases, 14
performance-based pay, 16
prerequisites, 15
skill-based pay, 16
stock options and bonuses, 15
supplemental pay systems, 15–16
"Cross-Sector Nonprofit Wage and
  Benefit Study," 3
cross-sector salary analysis and comparison results
  bookkeeper, 53–55
  clerk-typist, 60–62
  controller, 50–53
  department director, 47–50
  deputy director, 45–47
  executive director comparisons, 42–44
  gender comparison in nonprofit sector,
    40–41
  individual position comparisons, 41–62
  key findings, 37–38
  managerial/professional comparison,
    39
  office manager, 55–58
  by position, 38
  secretary, 58–60
  technical/clerical comparison, 39–40
cross-sector wages and benefits study,
  31–75
  common benchmark positions, 32–33
  data analysis, 36–37
  dollar-volume managed, 33–34
  federal pay systems, 33
  methodology, 31–37
  other comparison factors, 33–34
  salary analysis and comparison results,
    37–62
  survey data used, 34–36
Cumming, Charles M., 19

Day, Nancy E., 142
day care provisions, 84
defined-benefit pension, 71–72
defined-contribution pension, 72
"Delaware Nonprofit Wage & Benefit
  Survey, 1996 Edition," 151
department director, 184
  alternate position titles, 48
  cross-sector median and average
    annual salaries, 49
  cross-sector salary analysis and
    comparison results, 47–50
  key findings, 49–50
  nonprofit median salaries by gender, 49

position description, 47
salary data, 48–49
dependent care, 84
dependent life insurance, 67, 184
deputy director, 184
  alternate titles, 45
  cross-sector median and average
    annual salaries, 46
  cross-sector salary analysis and
    comparison results, 45–47
  key findings, 47
  nonprofit median salaries by gender,
    46
  position description, 45
  salary data, 45
direct compensation, 184
directors and compensation strategies, 14
disability, 67, 184
discretionary bonus plan case study
  background, 112–113
  criteria design checklist, 114
  plan elements summary, 113–114
Dunaway, Tim, 19

earned income, 11
employee, 184
Employment and Personnel: A Legal
  Handbook, 153
employment trends, 8–10
  executive wages, 9–10
  health care industry, 9
  labor union decline, 9
  manufacturing, 8
  nonprofit organizations, 10–12
  outsourcing, 9
  paid nonprofit employees, 10
  service industry, 9
  temporary help, 9
  underemployment, 9
  unemployment, 9
  wages decline, 9
  women, 10
excess benefit, 184
*Executive Compensation: A Primer for Board
  Members and Chief Executives,* 148–
  149
executive compensation by charitable
  organizations, 169–177
  intermediate sanctions, 173–176
  public concern, 170–171
  statutory framework, 171–173
executive director, 1, 184
  alternate position titles, 42

executive director *(continued)*
 cross-sector salary analysis and
  comparison results, 42–44
 key findings, 43–44
 nonprofit median salaries by gender,
  42
 position description, 42
 salary data, 43
executives
 compensation strategies, 14
 nonprofit compensation, 20–21
 SERPs (Supplemental Employee
  Retirement Programs), 14
executive wages and employment trends,
 9–10
extrinsic rewards, 19

federal pay systems, 33
Filipczak, Bob, 19
"Financial Incentives for Nonprofits," 25
financial stresses, 10–11
first steps in establishing compensation
 policy, 126–135
 human resources philosophy statement
  example, 127–128
 implementation, 135
 job-description format sample, 129–130
 preparation for developing policies,
  134–135
 recruiting compensation committee,
  132–133
 updating policies and practices, 135
first-time employees and implementing
 compensation plans, 136
flexible benefits plans, 65–66, 184
flexible spending accounts, 84
flextime/staggered hours, 84
for-profit companies
 compensation and other recruitment
  tools, 15
 developing their own employees, 21
 emphasis on individual achievement,
  20
 employees as company assets, 21–22
 extrinsic rewards, 19
 innovative compensation, 18–19
 intrinsic rewards, 19
 lump-sum payments, 15
 market pricing of jobs, 14
 merit increases, 14
 prerequisites, 15
 replacing employees, 14
 stock options and bonuses, 15

"Foundation Salary Report," 152
fund raisers, 185
 bonuses paid to, 25–26
 undervaluing, 26

gain sharing, 82, 185
government data, survey data used, 34–35
Gross, Steven E., 18

Hall, Holly, 25
Handbook of Leadership and Management,
 142
health benefits, 17
 definitions, 65–66
 flexible benefits plans, 65–66
 HMO (Health Maintenance Organization) plans, 65
 key findings, 66
 major medical plans, 65
 PPO (Preferred Provider Organization)
  plans, 65
help with compensation plans
 colleagues and contacts from similar
  organizations, 147–148
 related personnel issues resources,
  153–154
 resources, 148–149
 training and consultation sources, 155
 wage-and-benefit surveys, 149–153
Herman, Robert, 142
HMO (Health Maintenance Organization) plans, 65, 185
"How to Plan for Volunteer & Staff
 Success," 154
How to Write Job Descriptions, 154
human resource management, 4, 186
 system checklist, 123–124
human resources philosophy statement
 example, 127–128
*Human Resources Strategic Mandates for the
 1990s*, 22

immigrants, 8
implementing compensation plans, 121–
 122
 crossover employees, 137
 deciding on mix of types and
  strategies, 141
 determining eligibility, 141–142
 expert review of proposed plan, 142
 fair and competitive levels, 142
 first steps in establishing policy, 126–
  135

first-time employees, 136
formulating plan, 141–143
human resources management system
  checklist, 123–124
minority workers, 137–139
roles and relationships, 122–126
second careerists, 136–137
special considerations, 135–140
women, 136
incentive programs for nonprofit
  organizations, 20
indirect compensation, 185
individual incentives, 82, 185
innovative benefits, 63
innovative compensation, 17–19
  additional services, 21
  employee relations, 27
  extrinsic awards, 19
  incentives for motivating employees,
    19–20
  intrinsic awards, 19
  nonprofit companies, 20–22
  potential problems in nonprofit sector,
    25, 27
  recognition coupons, 19
innovative compensation plans
  benefit plans, 101–108
  case studies, 108–119
  discretionary bonus plan case study,
    112–114
  management incentive plan case study,
    108–112
  noncash recognition plan case study,
    117–119
  spot award plan case study, 114–117
innovative compensation practices, 79–
  119, 185
  analysis and findings, 84–108
  benefit plans, 84
  bonuses, 82
  cash-compensation or recognition
    plans, 89–101
  cash-compensation plans, 82–83
  day care provisions, 84
  definitions, 81–84
  dependent care, 84
  design implications, 92
  eligibility for, 87
  flexible spending accounts, 84
  flextime/staggered hours, 84
  gain sharing, 82
  general plan information, 87–89
  geographic areas, 86

individual incentives, 82
job-sharing, 84
length of design process, 89
lump sum increases, 83
need for information on, 79–80
number of employees, 86
number of survey participants, 87
objectives attempted to achieve, 87–88
participant profile, 85–86
predetermined performance objectives,
  82
premium conversion plan, 84
recognition plans, 82–83
required approvals, 89
skill-based pay, 83
special cash recognition, 83
special noncash recognition, 83
spot awards, 83
study methodology, 80–81
team or group incentives, 82
top management decisions about, 88–
  89
*Innovative Compensation Practices in the
  Nonprofit Sector,* 80
innovative compensation practices in the
  nonprofit sector, 185
"Innovative Compensation Practices in
  the Nonprofit Sector," xiii, 3
"intermediate sanction" provisions, 27,
  185
intrinsic rewards, 19
IOMA (Institute of Management
  Administration), 15, 185

job-sharing, 84
*The Jossey-Bass Handbook of Nonprofit
  Leadership and Management,* 149

401(k) plans, 72, 184
  new legislation, 165–166

"Labor Economics and the Nonprofit
  Sector: A Literature Review," 24
labor union decline, 9
Lawler, Edward, Ph.D., 19
Lawler, Edward E., III, 16
leadership, classification of, 4
leave benefits
  cross-sector benefits analysis and
    comparison results, 68–71
  key findings, 70–71
  miscellaneous leave, 69
  paid holidays, 69

leave benefits *(continued)*
  sick leave, 69
  vacation, 68–69
Ledford, Gerald E., Jr., 16
life and disability benefits, 66–68
  definitions, 67
  dependent life insurance, 67
  disability, 67
  key findings, 67–68
  life insurance, 67
  supplemental life insurance, 67
life insurance, 67, 186
lump sum increases, 83

major medical plans, 65, 186
management, classification of, 4
"1996 Management Compensation
  Report, Not-for-Profit Organizations," 150
management incentive plan case study,
  108–112
  background, 108–110
  design criteria checklist, 111–112
  plan elements summary, 110–111
managers, education, 10
manufacturing, 8
market pricing of jobs, 14, 186
McCullough, Lee, 18
men, 8
minority workers, 8
  implementing compensation plans,
  137–139
"Morale Coupons," 19
motivating employees, 22

"National Nonprofit Wage and Benefit
  Survey," 2
"1989 National Nonprofit Wage and
  Benefit Survey," 32
1990 National Survey of Executive
  Compensation, 20–21
new legislation for nonprofit organizations
  401(k) plans, 165–166
  other provisions affecting, 167
  SIMPLE (Savings Incentive Match Plan
  for Employees), 166–167
noncash recognition plan case study
  background, 117–118
  design criteria checklist, 119
  plan elements summary, 118–119
nonprofit management and leadership
  taxonomy, 186

advocacy, 157
ethics, 157–158
evaluation, 158
financial management, 158
general leadership, 159
general management, 159
governance, 159
human resource management, 159–160
information systems, 160
legal, 160–161
marketing, 161
operations management, 161–162
organization, design, and structure,
  162
planning, 162–163
resource development, 163
"Nonprofit Management and Leadership
  Taxonomy," 4
*The Nonprofit Management Handbook:
  Operating Policies and Procedures,* 148
nonprofit organizations, 186
  accidental death benefits, xii
  awareness of role of, 11
  bonuses, 15
  bonuses paid to fund-raisers, 25–26
  compensation practices, 3
  earned income, 11
  effectiveness, 2
  efficiency, 2
  employment rising, 22–23
  employment trends, 10–12
  executive compensation, 20–21
  financial stresses, 10–11
  functions, 2
  growth, 11
  health benefits, xii
  high executive pay, xi
  incentive programs, 20–22
  innovative compensation practices, 79–
  119
  leave policies, xii
  life insurance benefits, xii
  long-term disability benefits, xii
  low executive and employee pay, xi–xii
  new funding sources, 26
  profit-sharing pay systems, 16
  supplemental pay systems, 15–16
  survey data used, 34–35
Nonprofit Personnel Policies Manual, 154
Nonprofit Risk Management Center, 155
"1995 Nonprofit Salary and Benefits
  Survey of the Greater Kansas City
  Area," 150

nonprofit workers
  paid executive director, 1
  paid staff, 1
  volunteer board of directors, 1
  volunteers, 1–2
  "Not-for-Profit Salary Report, 1994-1995,"
    152

"Occupational Outlook Handbook," 8
O'Connell, Brian, xii–xiii, 23, 121
office manager, 186
  alternate position titles, 56
  cross-sector median and average
    annual salaries, 57
  cross-sector salary analysis and
    comparison results, 55–58
  key findings, 57–58
  nonprofit median salaries by gender,
    56
  position description, 55
  salary data, 56
older workers, 8
organization structure or infrastructure,
  186
outsourcing, 9

paid employees, 10, 186
paid holidays, 69
paid staff, 1
  benefits of well-designed compensa-
    tion packages, 3–4
pension plan, 187
Performance and Reward in Nonprofit
  Organizations: Evaluation, Compensa-
  tion, and Personnel Incentives, 25
performance-based pay, 16
Personnel Guide for Nonprofits, 154
Personnel Journal, 134
Personnel Policies and Procedures for
  Nonprofit Organizations, 154
Personnel Policies for Nonprofit Organiza-
  tions Nonprofit, 153
PPO (Preferred Provider Organization),
  187
PPO (Preferred Provider Organization)
  plans, 65
predetermined performance objectives,
  82
premium conversion plan, 84
private inurement, 187
professional employees
  education, 10
profit-sharing pay systems, 16

recognition plans, 89–101
  administration, 95
  award as separate check, 94
  baseline used, 95
  cash/noncash as form of award, 94
  changes in employee problem solving
    and/or decision making, 97
  changes in frequency of communica-
    tion, 96–97
  communication with plan participants,
    95–96
  compensation basis, 93
  definitions, 82–83
  design implications, 92
  funding, 99
  goal-level definitions, 99
  issues raised by, 99–101
  overview of survey results, 89–91
  participation, 99
  payouts as percentage of payroll, 92–
    93
  perceived favoritism, 100
  performance criteria, 95
  positive results, 97–98
  qualitative goals, 100
  substitution for other compensation
    elements, 93
  target award payouts, 93–94
  teamwork and collaboration, 92
  time between end of plan and payout,
    92
  types and findings, 91–97
  unexpected occurrences, 100
reimbursement accounts, 84
retirement benefits
  403(b) plan, 72–73
  cross-sector benefits analysis and
    comparison results, 71–73
  defined-benefit pension, 71–72
  defined-contribution pension, 72
  definitions, 71–72
  key findings, 73
  401(k) plan, 72
  supplemental executive plans, 73
"A Rewarding Place to Work," 19
reward systems
  components, 13
Rifkin, Jeremy, 9, 14
Rocco, James E., 179
roles and relationships, 122–126

"Salaries and Benefits in Youth Development Agencies," 151–152

salary, 187
Salary Management Planning Survey, 15
Samuels, David G., 169
second careerists
  implementing compensation plans,
    136–137
secretary, 187
  alternate position titles, 58
  cross-sector median and average
    annual salaries, 59
  cross-sector salary analysis and
    comparison results, 58–60
  key findings, 60
  nonprofit median salaries by gender,
    59
  position description, 58
  salary data, 58–59
SERPs (Supplemental Employee
  Retirement Programs), 14
SERP (Supplemental Employee Retirement Program), 187
sick leave, 69
SIMPLE (Savings Incentive Match Plan
  for Employees)
  new legislation, 166–167
skill-based pay, 16, 83
skilled-based pay, 187
The Society for Nonprofit Organizations,
  2
Society of Human Resource Management, 155
special cash recognition, 83
special noncash recognition, 83
spot award plan case study
  background, 114–116
  design criteria checklist, 117
  plan elements summary, 116–117
spot awards, 83
staff compensation, 1
Steinberg, Richard, 24, 27
stock options, 15
"Studies Document the Effects of Gender
  on Compensation," 15
supplemental executive plans, 73, 187
supplemental life insurance, 67, 187
"1995 Survey of New York Metropolitan
  Area Not-for-Profit Organizations,
  Compensation and ," 150

TAC (Technical Assistance Center), 2, 32
Taxpayer Bill of Rights 2, 179–182
team or group incentive, 188
team or group incentives, 82
teams, 19–20
temporary help, 9
"Tennessee Nonprofit Salary and Benefit
  Survey," 152
25th percentile, 188
training and consultation sources, 155

underemployment, 9
unemployment, 9

vacation, 68–69
volunteer board of directors, 1
volunteers, 1–2

"1996 Wage and Benefit Survey for
  Nonprofit Organizations," 152
wage-and-benefit surveys, 149–153
"Wage and Benefit Survey-Texas Gulf
  Coast Area," 153
"1996 Wage & Benefit Survey of
  Northern California Nonprofit
  Organizations," 150–151, 154
wages
  cross-sector analysis and comparison
    results, 37–62
  cross-sector study, 31–75
wages decline, 9
Wein, Jay, 25, 26
"Who Uses Skill-Based Pay, and Why,"
  16
women, 8
  implementing compensation plans, 136
  nonprofit organizations, 10
workforce
  employment trends, 8–10
  growth, 8
  men, 8
  minorities and immigrants, 8
  older workers, 8
  trends and demographics, 8
  women, 8
work unit, 188

Young, Dennis, 25